His Blood be Upon Us

Completion and Condemnation in Matthew's Gospel

By

Tom Wilson

His Blood be Upon Us: Completion and Condemnation in Matthew's Gospel

By Tom Wilson

This book first published 2022

Ethics International Press Ltd, UK

British Library Cataloguing in Publication Data

A catalogue record for this book is available from the British Library

Print Book ISBN: 978-1-80441-074-5

eBook ISBN: 978-1-80441-075-2

Table of Contents

Preface

There are two reasons why I decided to write this book. The first is that it provides me with an opportunity to reflect at length on one of the most complex sentences in Matthew's Gospel, the cry of "all the [Jewish] people" that "His blood be on us and on our children" (27:25). The second was seeing a photograph of a pro-Palestinian demonstration, held during May 2021, when conflict was raging across Israel-Palestine. One of those present at that demonstration held a placard with a drawing of Christ on the cross accompanied by the words "Don't let them do it again." The "them" referred presumably to Israelis or Jews or Israeli Jews. This is the charge of deicide, the killing of God, conflated with the blood libel, the claim Jewish people kill Christians in order to gather Christian blood to use in Jewish rituals, both of which have been levelled at Jewish people by Christians for centuries. The incident at the demonstration indicates that both charges are still present today. But are they justified? Were they ever justified? And how do we respond to both the long history of Christian persecution of Jewish people as well as the rise in contemporary antisemitism? Are there any plausible links between the "blood cry" of Matthew 27:25 and the so-called "blood libel" that began in 1150, and still resurfaces today? What about the issues of power and social standing that lie behind the text of Matthew's Gospel? How do we Christians, members of the world's biggest faith community, read and interpret words written when the first followers of Jesus were a tiny, embattled minority? As I will argue, the polemic of the text is the language of an embattled, scared, small group of followers of Jesus, responding to a perceived threat of attack or even extinction with every weapon they have, including vitriolic language. But how is that language to be taught and interpreted in our current context, where Christians are in the overwhelming majority vis-à-vis Jewish people? Exploring these issues is the task I have set myself in writing this book.

This is not the first time I have written at length about Christian antisemitism. In *Jesus and the Ioudaioi* (Wilson 2020) I explored how the Fourth Gospel portrays the *Ioudaioi*, variously translated as "Jews" or

"Judeans." The opening chapters of that book included a survey of Christian antisemitism down the centuries, and I will not repeat that general overview here. Indeed, I will reverse the trajectory of writing. *Jesus and the Ioudaioi* began with an overview and homed in on the Fourth Gospel. In this present volume, I will begin with Matthew's Gospel and then continue through history, discussing some of the occasions when the blood libel has been used as a pretext for the persecution and killing of Jewish people.

In a sense, the key question this book discusses is who does Matthew think is responsible for the death of Jesus. My answer is that it is Jesus himself, because three times he predicts his own death (16:21-23; 17:22-23; 20:17-19) and he acts provocatively and makes deliberate claims that invite his audience to conclude either he is divine or he is blaspheming. Jesus does this knowing that the punishment for blasphemy was death. Jesus also sets himself up as a rebel against the authority of the Roman Emperor and of Rome, and the penalty for such treason is also death. But ultimately, within the interpretative framework of Matthew's Gospel, Jesus is the fulfilment of the Jewish messianic hope, and he brings God's plan for the redemption of humanity to its intended goal through his own life, death and resurrection. It is Jesus who chooses death so that others may have life. Any charge of deicide is misplaced if it does not focus on these facts.

Yet this interpretation remains contested; the charge of deicide, and the arguably associated blood libel, have become enduring cultural tropes and excuses for discrimination, hatred and murder. The stark reality is that anti-Judaism and antisemitic hatred of Jewish people has a long and shameful history within Christianity, from the Church Fathers through Martin Luther, right up to the present day. Numerous Jewish scholars whose work I have read in preparation for writing cite their own, contemporary, experience of antisemitism. To give one example, when Levine was seven, she was accused of deicide:

> A friend on the school bus said to me, "You killed our Lord." "I did not," I responded with some indignation. Deicide would be the sort of thing I would have recalled. "Yes, you did," the girl insisted. "Our priest said so." Apparently, she had been taught that "the Jews"

were responsible for the death of Jesus. Since I was the only one she knew, I must be guilty (2006, 2).

How did an American Christian girl come to the conclusion her friend was a Christ-killer and/or a murderer of God? Because her religious leader taught her this was true. That may not have been the priest's intention, but it was the consequence of his actions. We must be aware of the damage our words can do.

At the conclusion to her discussion of Jesus as "the misunderstood Jew," Levine tells the story of Rebbe Moshe Leib of Sassov (1745-1807), who told his disciples that he had overheard a conversation between two villagers which taught him what it meant to love his neighbour. The first said, "Tell me, my friend, do you love me?" and the second replied that he loved his fellow deeply. The first responded, "Do you know what causes me pain?" and the second said that he did not. The answer came, "If you do not know what causes me pain, how can you say that you truly love me?" The rebbe's point was that to truly know what causes another pain is to truly love him (Levine 2006, 116-17). As a Christian, if I am to truly love my Jewish sisters and brothers, I must endeavour to understand how the faith I follow has caused them pain. That is my real purpose in writing this book.

There are eight main chapters in this book. The first chapter introduces some of the key academic debates about Matthew's Gospel. This sets the scene for the subsequent chapters that discuss aspects of the Gospel in more detail. Seven topics are covered: the nature of first-century Judaism; the genre of Matthew's Gospel; whether the primary focus of the Gospel is Rome; whether it was written before or after the destruction of the Jerusalem temple; whether the author resided in Antioch or Galilee; an overview of the "Matthew within Judaism" school of thought; and Bauckham's proposal that the Gospels were written for all Christians.

Chapter two explores what Matthew means by "fulfilment" in general and Jesus "fulfilling" the law in particular. After some orientation, the chapter begins with a note of caution from Levine and Brettler, two Jewish scholars of the New Testament. There follow the views of two groups: scholars of the "Matthew within Judaism" school, and six evangelical commentators, four scholarly and two popular. The "Matthew within Judaism" school is included for at least two reasons: it is a prominent group within the academic study of Matthew's Gospel and their concerns speak to the focus of this book, namely wrestling with Matthew's simultaneously pro- and anti-Jewish stance. Evangelical commentaries are discussed because they take the Gospel seriously, wanting to retain it as a normative sacred text whilst recognising the problems with many specific verses. A mix of scholarly and popular commentaries are utilised to explore how the problems are tackled at different levels.

Chapter three discusses the nature of first-century polemic, in seven parts. First, the nature of polemic is explored. Second, the polemic of the Hebrew Scriptures and third, in the New Testament is discussed. Fourth, Overmann's selection of other non-canonical polemical texts is introduced. Fifth, Kampen's proposal of reading Matthew as a sectarian document is analysed. Sixth, the option of simply regarding Matthew as polemic is rejected, through recognition that the Gospel is a normative sacred text for billions of people, and seventh a more robust and nuanced response is explored.

The purpose of the discussion of polemic is to outline the context for the discussion of Matthew 23 in chapter four. Matthew 23 contains a sustained polemic against the Pharisees, spoken by Jesus, and as such is an important part of the wider discussion. How are Christians to respond to Jesus' harsh language in this chapter? Having situated the Pharisees historically, the chapter discusses four interpretative approaches to the text; the inter-faith focused approach of Hilton and Marshall; the discussion of the Pharisees by Yarbro-Collins and others; the views of some members of the Matthew within Judaism school; and the six evangelical views introduced in chapter three. The main conclusion is that for the Matthew within Judaism school, the polemic is interpreted as the beleaguered Matthean community defending itself by any means possible. For the evangelical Christian scholars any modern application of the polemic should be internally focused, that is, directed against oneself and one's fellow Christians.

Chapter five focuses on a single verse, the "blood cry" of Matthew 27:25, one of the most challenging verses of the New Testament, that is at the root of the charge of deicide which has impacted Jewish people terribly down the centuries. The chapter has six parts: some cautionary words from Amy-Jill Levine; the narrative-critical approach of Heil; Sider-Hamilton's discussion of innocent blood; Konradt's exploration of the role of crowds; the Matthew within Judaism school; and the six evangelical perspectives. The main issue discussed is how this text is explained and interpreted by contemporary scholars, concluding the most common approach is to limit the scope to the crowd and their immediate children. These scholars lament the impact of interpretation that gave greater scope to the reference; but is this enough? It is all very well to recognise the charge of deicide is founded on an inaccurate interpretation of Matthew 27:25, but do preachers and teachers speak out against this falsehood?

Chapter six explores whether there is a connection between the blood cry and subsequent blood libels against Jewish people. The chapter proposes that anti-Jewish readings of Matthew's Gospel, especially 27:25, provided the foundations on which subsequent Christian antisemitism was built. In essence, the proposal is that if it was believed the Jews killed Jesus, then Christians expected Jews to try and kill them also. This appears to be the perspective of Thomas of Monmouth, the monk at Norwich Cathedral who first popularised and spread the blood libel. After discussing the Norwich case, there follows a brief history of blood libels down the ages, including exploration of incidents in Damascus, Kiev and Massena, New York, in more detail, noting the culpability of Christians in spreading these lies. The conclusion notes the blood libel is still spread today, even in Jerusalem.

Chapter seven explores ways Christians can preach from Matthew's Gospel with Jewish people in mind. Five proposals are introduced: the importance of acknowledging supersessionism; ways of removing anti-Judaism from the pulpit; the evangelical blogger Ian Paul's proposals on "how to not be antisemitic"; Harrington's suggestions in relation to Matthew's Gospel; and Jewish scholar of the New Testament Amy-Jill Levine's "alphabet of suggestions" for good Jewish-Christian relations. The purpose of the chapter is to provide opportunity for reflection on how to remain a faithful Christian teacher and preacher without being antisemitic.

Chapter eight consists of four sample sermons that demonstrate how the concerns raised in this book can be incorporated into public teaching. The texts discussed are Matthew 5:17-20; 16; 23 and 27:25. These sermons are simply examples, my own limited attempts at preaching with Jewish people in mind. They are aids to reflection, and are in no way definitive.

The postscript revisits the question of who killed Jesus, drawing together the threads of the whole discussion. I am particularly grateful to Dr Uri Gordon, and to other Jewish and Christian friends and colleagues for their insights, advice and guidance given to earlier drafts of this book. Much that is good in this book is down to them. Any errors, of omission or commission, remain entirely my own.

Chapter 1
When, Where, and Why was Matthew's Gospel Written?

One of the preoccupations of scholars of the New Testament is determining the occasion and provenance of the texts under scrutiny. That is to say, working out when, where and why they were written. There are no certainties in this quest, only probabilities, and there is a danger of circular arguments. One example of this process is where a certain feature of the text is identified as indicating a particular date of composition, and then on the basis of that feature, the date of composition is concluded. In Matthew's Gospel, the most often-cited verse in this regard is 22:7, which is taken as indicating the text *must* have been written after the destruction of the Jerusalem temple in 70 CE. In the midst of the parable of the wedding banquet, the king, whose invitation has been scorned, sends his troops who "destroyed those murderers and burnt their city." As shall become clear below, the majority view amongst scholars is that this is a direct reference to the destruction of Jerusalem and its temple, and so must have been written after those events occurred.

In what follows, I begin with a few points of orientation about first-century Judaism. Second, Donald Hagner's discussion of the nature of Matthew's Gospel is introduced. Third, Warren Carter's arguments in favour of a Roman-focus is evaluated. Fourth, the date, place of composition and focus of the text of Matthew is discussed, taking in the views of John Nolland, Aaron Gale, Craig Keener, Anthony J Saldarini, John Kampen and J Andrew Overman. Finally, some words of caution about the "Matthew within Judaism" school and an examination of Bauckham's "Gospel for all Christians" argument draw the threads together. The aim of this chapter is to familiarise the reader with some relevant academic debates within the study of Matthew's Gospel.

First-century Judaism

There have been many attempts at reconstructing the Judaism (or Judaisms) of the first-century CE. Two recent notable projects by Protestant Christian writers are the work of Dunn (2003, 2006) and Wright (1993, 1997, 2003). Dunn argues that although there is evidence of diversity, most people followed what he terms "common Judaism," which means Judaism as defined by the "Four Pillars" of Second Temple Judaism. Dunn explains these as monotheism; the election of Israel; covenant focused on Torah; and land focused on temple. Second Temple Jewish monotheism was absolute, denying the divine any partners or rivals. Israel was an elect nation, chosen by God to receive divine self-revelation. The Torah was given to Israel as part of God's covenant with Israel, and obedience to the Law of Moses was Israel's response to God's choice of Israel to be his people. The temple was the centre of Israel's economic, religious and political life, with the High Priest having as much a political as a religious function and the economic impact of temple festivals having as great a significance as their religious impact (see Dunn 2003, 286-92; 2006, 24-48 for more on these "four pillars").

Neusner explains that "Jesus came into a world of irrepressible conflict. That conflict was between two pieties, two universal conceptions of what the world required." That is to say, there was a clash between the Roman and Jewish understandings of the world. Roman government demanded a *pax Romana,* Roman rule, Roman imposed peace, with its blessings of civil order and material prosperity. As part of this commitment, they could never leave Palestine, which was the corner of a major trade route between Egypt and Asia Minor. But for Jewish people, who believed "history depended on what happened in the Land of Israel," and in particular what took place in Jerusalem, Israel needed to be free of Roman rule and focused on serving the Lord God (1984, 32-33). In a subsequent book, Chilton and Neusner (1995) are at pains to establish clear connections between Jesus and his Jewish contemporaries, whilst also pointing to their differences.

In her discussion of the birth of Christianity and the origins of Christian anti-Judaism, Fredriksen notes that Pagans who joined Judaism did so "on an individual, voluntary, ad hoc, and improvised basis" (2002, 14). She explains that Jews did not actively reach out in mission because they were worried about making themselves unpopular. Fredriksen elaborates:

> Extremely tolerant of those outside the fold, Jews were rancorously, almost exuberantly, intolerant of variety within the fold. Battling with each other over the correct way to be Jewish was (one could say, is) a timeless Jewish activity, and at no time more so than in the late Second Temple period, precisely the lifetime of Jesus and Paul (2002, 15).

The debate within Second Temple Judaism was not over whether to fulfil the law, but how to do so. The controversies that Jesus gets embroiled in are therefore part-and-parcel of a wider, intra-Jewish debate about Torah obedience. The particular issue for Christians who are reading the New Testament today is therefore how to explain that the New Testament is full of intra-Jewish polemic but at the same time recognise that polemic can be read as a condemnation of Judaism itself (Fredriksen 2002, 14-18). Whilst it is factually accurate to observe that debates within first-century Judaism were polemical, this is insufficient in dealing with the history of Christian anti-Judaism and antisemitism that have their origins in the texts of the New Testament in general, and Matthew's Gospel in particular. A more robust approach must be taken. But before making suggestions as to what that approach might look like, it is important to first get the context clear.

Who was arguing?

Whilst today we talk in terms of Christians and Jews, those terms are much more slippery when used in the context of Second Temple Judaism. As Kampen explains:

> It is not clear that we can speak of something called "Judaism" in the first century CE in the same way that we speak of a Judaism or Christianity today, in which we compare systems of belief with some attention to resultant practices. I do not, however, think that the attempts prevalent in the 1990s to talk about "Judaisms" adequately resolved the problem for the analysis of Jewish history, since they

simply assumed that there are multiple systems of belief. At the heart of the matter, as discussed in this volume, the debate is over practices and affiliation rather than belief and theology: Whose temple do you enter? Whose assemblies do you frequent? What practices do they have that you observe, and what is the rationale behind them? (2019, 3).

The question is thus primarily about loyalty and belonging. Behaviour defines membership of both in-group and out-group. With whom was Matthew arguing and how did those engaged in the debate understand themselves and those they were engaging with? How were these differences elucidated by the way in which people behaved, by which religious rites and practices they observed, and which they abstained from?

In his book *Borderlines*, Boyarin argues that the borders "between Christianity and Judaism are as constructed and imposed, as artificial and political as any of the borders on earth" (2004, 1). He uses a geo-political analogy to illustrate his point that there was no single incident that led to a definitive parting of the ways between Christianity and Judaism, but a partitioning of what was a territory without border lines, as with Indian and Pakistan or Israel and Palestine. Boyarin continues:

The border space between the juridical and abstract entities Judaism and Christianity, throughout late antiquity and even beyond, was a crossing point for people and religious practices (2004, 1).

Boyarin argues that those trying to create the borders created the notion of heresiology and so reinforced the very division they were policing (2004, 2-3). Although Matthew does not use the word heresy, it is clear that, if we follow Boyarin's view that orthodoxy and heresy are not things, but notions that are defined against each other, then at least one function of Matthew's Gospel is to distinguish between what he regards as orthodox, that is, an accurate interpretation of how God is at work in the world, and what is not.

The challenges come in discerning the interplay between the neat division between in-group and out-group Matthew tries to provide, and the messy reality of what people actually believed and did. That is to say, first-century

Christianity and Judaism should not be thought of as monolithic entities, but rather as amorphous groupings that had clear enough cores, but whose external borders were fuzzy rather than concrete. As he develops his argument, Boyarin uses the analogy of colour, suggesting that we contrast Christianity and Judaism in the first century with categories such as red or tall, rather than more fixed groupings such as bird or fish. That is to say, an item could be more or less red, more or less tall, but something is either a bird or it is not. In the same way, someone could be more or less Christian, but this is a graded, rather than an absolute, distinction (2004, 25).

Boyarin's focus is primarily the period after the New Testament was written, but his observations are just as salient for this period. He explains that "the difference between Christianity and Judaism is not so much a difference between two religions as a difference between a religion and an entity that refuses to be one" (2004, 8). Boyarin adds that the term "Judaism" in reference to a religion only really comes into being in the nineteenth century. Boyarin concludes:

> In the end, it is not the case that Christianity and Judaism are two separate or different religions, but that they are two different kinds of things altogether. From the point of view of the Church's category formation, Judaism and Christianity (and Hinduism later on) are examples of the category *religions*, one a bad example and the other a very good one, indeed the only prototype. But from the point of view of the Rabbis' categorization, Christianity is a religion and Judaism is not. Judaism remains a religion for the Church because, I will suggest, it is a necessary moment in the construction of Christian orthodoxy and thus Christian religion, whereas occasional and partial Jewish appropriations of the name and status of religion are strategic, mimetic and contingent" (2004, 13).

Boyarin's contention is that the Church defined Judaism as a religion purely for internal purposes of self-definition; that is to say, one way in which Christians defined the borders of their religion in the first few centuries was to be categorical about who was excluded. This desire, to define "Christian" as "not-Jewish," is a dangerous move, especially when Christians have most, if not all, of the power.

The point to particularly bear in mind throughout this study is that we bring our own unconscious biases to the analysis of the text. Christians should be wary of presuming to know what Judaism is, what Jewish people believe, and how Matthew's Gospel is heard by Jewish people. We presume we know more about those who are not like us than is, in fact, the case. A particularly serious example of this is the tendency to presume the New Testament's portrayal of Jewish people must be accepted entirely at face value. Moreover, we must be careful in presuming to know what different words mean, or the intention behind use of polemic or confrontational language. Alternative meanings must be considered, and the function of language considered carefully. As Boyarin points out, a more nuanced, self-reflexive approach is needed.

What sort of text is Matthew's Gospel?

Recognition of genre is important when reading a text; to give a simple example, a letter from a solicitor will use different language from a letter from a spouse. Most genres have stylistic conventions; if we know the genre, the task of interpreting the text becomes simpler. This is a true for New Testament texts as it is for any other writing.

Hagner identifies seven possible genres for the Gospel of Matthew. It might be classed as a gospel, that is, as an account of the life of Jesus. But it might also be described as a midrash, "setting forth an edifying, theological interpretation of Jesus in, or under the form of, historical narrative." Third, it might be a lectionary to supplement the Jewish festival year. Fourth, a catechetical manual, perhaps for a so-called Matthean school of Christian instruction. Fifth, was Matthew's Gospel written to provide corrective guidance to a community under pressure? Or sixth, is it primarily missionary propaganda, particularly with the purpose of persuading Jews that Jesus is the Messiah? Finally, it might be a polemic against the rabbis, particularly in the context of the destruction of the Jerusalem Temple in 70 CE (1993, lvii-lix).

There is no particular reason to settle on only one of these alternatives; Matthew's Gospel may well fulfil many, if not all, of these functions. The point is simply to note that the text functions in a variety of ways. When we read the Gospel, or extracts from the Gospel, a helpful place to begin is to decide what type of text we are reading, what was Matthew's intention in writing it, and where is his focus.

Is Matthew focused primarily on Rome?

If we have some ideas as to what type of text Matthew's Gospel is, the next question is, where is his focus when writing? Warren Carter is a New Testament scholar who reads the texts primarily through the lens of the Roman Empire. Thus he argues:

> Matthew's plot is an act of imperial negotiation. Unfolding in six stages, its central dynamic comprises conflict between Jesus and the Rome-allied (Jerusalem based) leaders. It ends with God raising Jesus, crucified by an imperial elite (2007, 424).

In Carter's reading, the Jewish authorities are proxies for Rome, and thus Jesus' mission is primarily to repair the damage that Rome has done to Israel. A typical example is Carter's interpretation of the payment of the temple tax. Carter notes that Jesus instructs Peter to pay the half-shekel temple tax with a coin found in the mouth of a fish (17:24-27). Before the destruction of the Temple in 70 CE, this tax was paid to the Temple authorities. But after the Temple was no more, the Emperor Vespasian co-opted the payments, using it to fund rebuilding and maintenance costs of the temple of Jupiter Capitolinus in Rome. This reminded the Jews not only of Rome's military might, but also of the supposed superiority of Jupiter against the God of Israel. In Carter's interpretation, Matthew's account of the incident is written after 70 CE, and thus Jesus "reframes an action intended to humiliate by attributing to it a different significance that dignifies the dominated and attests to God's sovereignty, not Rome's" (2007, 430). Equally, in Carter's reading of the Passion Narrative, it is Pilate who manipulates the Jerusalem based religious leaders into begging him to crucify Jesus. Matthew, Carter contends, exposes this strategy of the doomed Roman empire ranged against Jesus the agent of God's empire (2007, 432-33).

Although Carter defends his argument well, it is out of step with the current majority view on the purpose of Matthew. Most scholars focus primarily on the idea of Matthew within Judaism, rather than Matthew focused against Rome. Despite not being widely taken up, Carter's view is an important corrective to the presumption that Matthew is solely focused on an intra-Jewish debate. Although I do think Matthew does want to argue with his fellow Jews about the identity of Jesus of Nazareth, that does not mean he had no concern for gentiles or the Roman empire. The language of the "kingdom of the heavens" that is so common in Matthew is aimed at multiple audiences.

Was Matthew written before the destruction of the Temple?

Rome was the occupying military power in the Palestine of Jesus' day, and when Matthew was written. But there is a debate as to precisely when in that occupation Matthew wrote. In what follows, I set out two arguments for a relatively early date of composition. John Nolland argues that Matthew was written prior to the Jewish war that led to the destruction of the Jerusalem temple in 70 CE. This means he is confident that the traditions which lie behind the Gospel text, if not the Gospel text itself, were produced at a time when there were eyewitnesses to Jesus' life and ministry who were themselves still alive (2005, 12-13).

The main reason for his scepticism is that the text of Matthew's Gospel does not, in his view, contain anything that anchors it specifically in the 80s or 90s CE, nor do the supposed hints of knowledge of destruction of the temple (22:7; 23:36, 38 and 24:2) indicate anything that means we must believe them to have been written after that event occurred. In Nolland's understanding, New Testament critical scholarship only identifies as "genuine" those alleged prophecies which are not fulfilled, and any apparent prophecy that has been fulfilled is argued by those who hold this view to actually have been composed after the event. Nolland rejects this scepticism. He acknowledges the prophecy in 22:7 might have been "touched up" after the fall of Jerusalem, but is clear that it is an "un-called for imposition" to presume the destruction of Jerusalem and the Temple could not have been predicted before the events occurred (2005, 14).

Nolland himself is sceptical about identification of the precise situation faced by the Matthean community. He argues that there were many rifts within first-century Judaism, and that the mutual hostility which characterised these divisions means we cannot be sure precisely what the hostility towards the Pharisees in chapter twenty-three indicates about the situation faced by Matthew and his fellow followers of Jesus. It is possible that the Matthean Christians had their own synagogues, but that might equally be true of other Jewish groups. There is, Nolland points out, no clear plan or record of the split between Christianity and Judaism, and as such we cannot know where precisely to place Matthew within that larger frame (2005, 15-16). He concludes:

> More broadly, the lack of precision in Mt. 24 and the limitation of a precise fit between the materials in Mt. 24 and first-century events between the time of Jesus and the outcome of the Jewish war make it likely that Matthew reports prophecy before the event, and not prophecy after the event, as so often maintained (2005, 16).

For Nolland, then, Matthew is an early composition, with not much to say about the situation faced by Matthew, and his fellow followers of Jesus.

Quarles (2021) argues in favour of a pre-70 date for Matthew primarily on the basis of the "oath formulae" of Matthew 23:16-22. This passage consists of a polemical condemnation of the scribes and Pharisees (described here as "blind guides") for permitting people to swear on the basis of different aspects of the temple (the gold held in the sanctuary, the gift on the altar). Quarles notes that these particular types of oaths are rare to non-existent after the destruction of the temple, which makes good sense, as who would make an oath on the basis of something that no longer exists? Quarles then extrapolates from this evidence to suggest that for the polemic of Matthew 23:16-22 to have the desired rhetorical impact on those with whom the Matthean Jesus-followers were debating, the temple must still be standing and the oaths must still have some validity. That is to say, if an oath sworn on the temple loses its force once the temple is destroyed, why reference the fact that your opponent permits such oaths if they no longer, in fact, do so? Since these oaths were only sworn while the temple was still standing, that therefore implies that Matthew's Gospel was written the temple existed, that is, before 70 CE.

As with Carter's argument above, this case for an early date has not convinced the majority of scholars, who are more persuaded by a post-70 date for the composition of the text. Personally, I think Nolland and Quarles make some worthwhile points, and so I am open to the possibility that the final form, or a near final form, of the Gospel was written before the destruction of the temple. I do recognise that presumption of a later date is useful for mirror reading the context of the so-called "Matthean community" from the text of the Gospel. But this process is entirely speculative, and so although it is a useful interpretative strategy, it must not be held too tightly. The same can also be said of the debate as to the place of composition, where the two main contenders are Syrian Antioch and Galilee.

Antioch or Galilee?

Aaron Gale argues that the Matthean community were followers of Jesus who also observed the stipulations of Torah, and were based in Sepphoris in Galilee. He argues that Judaism in Palestine after 70 CE was in turmoil – no wealth, no temple, forced exile. One of the two cornerstones of the faith (the temple) had been destroyed, and so the leaders of Judaism, the rabbis, gathered in Yavneh to reformulate Judaism focused on the other cornerstone, the Torah. In Gale's reconstruction, Palestinian Judaism maintained a coherent form during this process of reformulation, in both the Jerusalem region and in Galilee. Gale's focus is on what happened in Galilee, where he argues there was a revival of Jewish practice and thought. But it wasn't all plain sailing. There were complaints about those who were not observing Torah, which Gale suggests is a reference to Jewish Christians.

Gale's argument is that the scribes who wrote Matthew's Gospel were in conflict with those who were attempting to reshape Judaism centred primarily on the Torah. Both groups were active in Galilee towards the end of the first century CE, and both were competing for leadership of the Jewish community in the region. This is why Jesus talks about fulfilling the law in Matthew 5:17-48; 23. Both the Hebrew Scriptures and the Talmud teach that it is prohibited to add or subtract anything from the Torah. "Simply put, Matthew and formative Judaism were fighting over the Torah" (2005, 31).

Gale gives four reasons for regarding Matthew's Gospel as a thoroughly Jewish text. First, all the titles used are Jewish (apart from "apostles" in 10:2). Second, only Jewish speakers refer to Jesus as "teacher," while Gentiles call him "Christ" or "Son of God." Third, Jesus is in discussion with Jewish religious leaders, for example the scribes and Pharisees of 12:38. Fourth, Jesus himself makes extensive use of the Hebrew scriptures. The picture Gale constructs is of a group of Torah-observant Jews, who have also become convinced that Jesus of Nazareth is the promised messiah, gathered in a major urban centre in Galilee, such as Sepphoris. This group is in regular dialogue – and dispute – with other groups of Jews, especially those who are reconstructing Judaism to be primarily Torah focused after the destruction of the Temple in 70 CE. Gale discusses the scholarly contention that the community which produced Matthew's Gospel was based in Antioch, and dismisses the hypothesis on at least four grounds. First, he argues that even in the Galilee, Jews did speak Greek, and so the language of the Gospel does not preclude a Galilean origin. Second, Gale proposes that Antioch was probably too big to serve as a base for the Matthean community to be the only Christian presence; in his view, Sepphoris was a more suitable size. Third, whilst it is true that Matthew 4:15 refers to "Galilee of the Gentiles," this phrase is unique in both Matthew and Isaiah, whom Matthew is quoting. Far from indicating that the region was predominantly Gentile, it indicates Matthew's reinterpretation of Isaiah's messianic hope that all nations would come under the influence of the God of Israel. Fourth, and finally, Matthew's Gospel focuses on Jesus' ministry in Galilee. Gale argues that Matthew was written in Sepphoris, the most important city in the region at that time (2005, 1-63).

As he develops his hypothetical reconstruction of the Matthean community, Gale argues that it was wealthy, citing evidence of flourishing Galilean commerce, involving agriculture, fishing and potentially the book trade. Moreover, Matthew refers more to wealth than the other Gospels. The debtor in Matthew 18:23 owes ten thousand talents (in contrast with Luke 7:41's mention of five hundred denarii); Jesus approves of the Temple tax, mentioning coins unique to Matthew (the two-drachma coin, 17:24 and the shekel, 17:27); and curses the Pharisees for their oaths sworn on the gold of the sanctuary (23:16-17). Finally, the parable in which slaves are tested by being given wealth has a far more valuable denomination (talents) than in Luke (who uses pounds) as can be seen by contrasting Luke 19:11-27 with Matthew 25:14-30 (Gale 2005, 64-76).

Kampen supports Gale's argument, explaining that

> The gospel of Matthew demands a provenance that was Jewish and included representatives of some of the sectarian groups found in the Jewish communities at the end of the first century or their successors. That Jewish community was located in an urban environment, most likely somewhere in Galilee in the Roman province of Syria, since that is the area which would have had the most proximity to the kinds of sectarian groups mentioned in Matthew and present in Judea in the first century, particularly as they are described in Josephus. The use of the Greek language also points to an urban environment and to a significant role for that Jewish community within it. The author presumed not only an immediate circle of devotees but a wider circle of Jewish readers and hearers (2019, 20).

In Kampen's view, although other locations are possible, Galilee is the most persuasive possibility.

Whilst Gale and Kampen favour Galilee as the place of composition of Matthew's Gospel, others are unsure. Craig Keener recognises that we can reconstruct some of the basic details of the context that Matthew is writing in response to, but that any detailed proposals are necessarily speculative. He is comfortable with Antioch as location for the Matthean Community. He recognises the evidence is meagre and suggests it was

> an urban center in Syro-Palestine that spoke Greek, included a sizable Jewish community residentially separated from Gentiles, probably remained bitter against the Romans for the recent massacres of 66-70, and remained in touch with rising currents in Judea (1999, 42).

Thus, Keener adopts the more established view of composition in Antioch in the 70s or 80s of the first century.

In his discussion of the situation addressed by Matthew's Gospel, Keener welcomes the corrective influence of Bauckham's "Gospel for all Christians" proposal that rejects the detailed reconstruction of specific communities targeted by a particular Gospel. But at the same time, Keener argues that Matthew does have particular emphases and allusions that suggest a largely Jewish audience. He suggests that modern concepts of a "target audience" or "market niche" might provide a useful framework for understanding that when we refer to a "community" this does not mean a single house church or movement within a city, but rather a broad focus (1999, 45). Keener suggests that Matthew particularly targets the successors of the scribes and the Pharisees, that is the "founders of the rabbinic movement at Jamnia and whatever Jewish leaders throughout Syro-Palestine may have been aligned with or influenced by them" (1999, 46). Keener explains that Matthew, like Jesus, agreed with some of the Pharisees' teaching but disapproved of their behaviour. Keener adds that there is no need to reference the *birkat-ha-minim*, the "curse against heretics" that tradition held was promulgated by the rabbis at Yavneh in the 70s CE. Support for this understanding has faded in recent years, and Keener is typical in preferring to imagine a general tone of opposition and distrust, rather than an organised opposition grouping, as the likely backdrop against which Matthew wrote (1999, 46-47).

Keener is agnostic as to whether the Matthean Christians had severed all contact with the synagogue, but is clear that they held themselves apart as a distinct grouping (1999, 48). He explains

> I find in the Gospel an author and audience intensely committed to their heritage in Judaism while struggling with those they believe to be its illegitimate spokespersons (1999, 49).

It is important to remember that leaving the synagogue in the first-century is not like switching church allegiance in the twenty-first. Being expelled from or choosing to leave the synagogue meant leaving your whole social world and family, cutting oneself off from all relationships of social and economic dependence.

In his conclusion to the introduction of his commentary, Keener explains that the evidence from both Matthew and John supports the idea that Jesus was a popular figure in the first-century, even after his death, and that his followers were still respected in Galilee. But there was an emerging threat: the successors to the Pharisees were emerging as a rival dominant force, with a different understanding of the nature of authentic Judaism. Although this group was not yet powerful, it had sufficient traction with the intelligentsia and influencers of the day that Jewish Christians began to feel threatened by them. Thus, as the debate developed between the numerous but relatively powerless Jewish Christians and the smaller group of Pharisaic elites, Matthew wrote his text to equip his readers with ready responses to the Jewish legal scholars with whom they disagreed, as well as to encourage them to devote their energies to the mission to the gentiles, as a precursor to the expected repentance of all Israel. In this situation, facing persecution, false prophets, apostasy and the need for more workers, Matthew writes to encourage the church to faithfully follow Jesus (1999, 70).

Although Keener's reconstruction is attractive, I am not completely convinced by it. As we will see below, it is difficult to provide clear evidence of continuity from first-century Pharisees to subsequent rabbinic Judaism. We simply do not know anything concrete about Matthew's own situation either. It is likely he faced opposition; it is certain that Jesus did, as Jesus' crucifixion is one of the few certainties in this whole debate. Much of the rest is down to a balance of probabilities.

It is impossible to be sure when or where Matthew's Gospel was written. As noted above, I can see the strengths of the case for a pre-70 date of composition, but also note the majority view of a later date, and the interpretative strategies that are built on that presumption. Regarding place of composition, I find Gale and Kampen's view marginally more persuasive than Keener's. This is partly because of where and how the Gospel ends (in Galilee, with the disciples sent out from there) and partly because recognition of a potentially earlier date makes Galilee all the more plausible. But in the end, there is no certainty and whichever options are chosen does not impact the argument of this book that much. A more pressing concern is the relationship between Matthew and the Jewish community, to which I now turn.

Matthew within Judaism

There is a trend within recent scholarship of Matthew to locate the text primarily within Judaism. As will be seen below, this is not entirely unproblematic, but is nevertheless a useful thought experiment. Anthony Saldarini is one scholar who takes this approach. Saldarini explains his position as follows: that Matthew and his community

> are Jews who believe in Jesus as Messiah and Son of God. The Matthean group is a fragile minority still thinking of themselves as Jews and still identified with the Jewish community by others. Despite its sharp conflicts with the leaders of the Jewish community and its experience of standard disciplinary measures, or better, because of these negative relationships, the Matthean group is still Jewish (1994, 1).

He adds that such experiences of rejection do not necessarily drive a minority group away; in this case, as in others, being labelled as deviant actually encourages adherence to the main group. Saldarini also rejects classification as "Christian" as anachronistic, and a category error, and rejects an approach that only listens to the voice of the majority, dominant group. Saldarini argues that what groups say about themselves and others often reflects what they wish was true, rather than what is actually true. Thus, Matthew's group have recently withdrawn from or been expelled by the majority Jewish community, but they still have close symbolic and actual ties with the main group. Matthew hopes that one day his view will become the majority one within the Jewish community (1994, 1-2).

For Saldarini, Matthew's Gospel speaks to two worlds, both the developing Christian theology that flourished in the second century, and also the Jewish debate as to how to live and practise faith in the aftermath of the destruction of the temple. He argues that the Gospel is "an integral and coherent whole reflecting a Christian-Jewish group which keeps the whole law, interpreted through the Jesus tradition" (1994, 7). The purpose of the Gospel is to promote Matthew's understanding of Judaism over against any other views. But this is not an exclusionary approach, as

> members of the Jewish community who reject Jesus, especially the leaders, are excoriated in the prophetic mode as unfaithful members of Israel, but members nonetheless. Israel is the concrete community of Jews from which Matthew has been banned, but to which he still thinks he belongs (1994, 7).

This means Matthew must be located within first-century Judaism rather than as external or in opposition towards it. Saldarini argues that first-century Judaism was highly diverse, not centralised or monolithic as is sometimes presumed. The first followers of Jesus were Jewish and operated within Judaism. The process of separation was gradual and took generations; it was only starting to take place at the time Matthew was written. Christians and Jews continued to compete for followers and position within wider society for several hundred years, into the fourth century. Saldarini notes, for example, that John Chrysostom perceived

Judaism to be a threat in fourth-century Antioch. Far from seeing the development of Christianity as uniform and smooth, Saldarini argues it was uneven and complex, and that there is evidence of these differences even in the pages of the New Testament. The Gospel of Mark, which he argues was written in the 70s of the first-century has a subtly different perspective on many questions vis-à-vis the Gospel of Matthew, never mind the views of other, non-canonical texts. Saldarini concludes that both rabbinic Judaism and the Jesus movement began as reformist groups within Judaism. The former flourished across the Roman Empire and Mesopotamia, reforming existing Jewish communities, whilst the latter came to focus primarily on gentiles, and so became an independent religion. Despite a growth in anti-Jewish attitudes, good relations also persisted. For Saldarini it is unnecessary to posit a sharp division between "Jews" and "Christians" at the time Matthew's Gospel was written (1994, 11-26).

Overman's views are similar to those of Saldarini. In Overman's reading of the setting and context in which Matthew's Gospel was written, Matthew and his fellow disciples of Jesus were in dispute with the Pharisees and the scribes over what constituted authentic Judaism in the wake of the destruction of the temple. Overman believes that this debate lurks just below the surface of the text of the First Gospel. Thus, the scribes and the Pharisees represent those who challenge the Matthean Community over their interpretation of the law, they are the yardstick by which Matthew defines pious and just behaviour and they plot against Jesus. In Overman's reconstruction, the Pharisees and the Matthean community both have gatherings (in *synagoge* and *ecclesia* respectively), both had authoritative teachers and devoted disciples, and both were seeking to fill the vacuum left by the destruction of the temple (1996, 12-16). Overman concludes that the scribes and Pharisees "were the legendary bad boys in Matthew's world. Matthew's church viewed these people not just as rivals, but as threats to their safety and way of life." Perhaps, Overman suggests, some had even started leaving the Matthean church in favour of the Pharisees, and is this exodus the Gospel is written to stop (1996, 20).

The main contention of the "Matthew within Judaism" school is just that; Matthew's Gospel much be read as part of an intra-Jewish argument. This is useful in developing a response to the polemic found in the text, but it is not without problems of its own.

Some words of caution

Whilst there has been a strong push in some recent scholarship to reconstruct a hypothetical Matthean community and mirror read that community's experience from the text of the Gospel, this is an imaginative exercise that can potentially go too far.

Amy-Jill Levine comments that it is incorrect to argue that the "entire Jewish world" was in alliance against Jesus and his followers. In her view, it is more accurate to compare the Jewish leadership with other elites, whether the Roman rulers, or Jesus' disciples who become too certain of their own importance or even "those who attempt to control the church through domination rather than those who guide through service" (1988, 99).

We must be aware of the danger of reading our prejudices and biases into the text. Having said that, it is clear that Matthew is a problematic text. As France puts it, "Perhaps the central problem in the study of Matthew's gospel is how to make sense of the apparently inconsistent attitude towards Judaism which the gospel displays" (1989, 95).

France notes there are all kinds of pointers towards a Jewish-focus of Matthew's gospel, including transliterated Aramaic words (*raka*, 5:22, *mammon*, 6:24, *korban*, 27:6); reference to details of Jewish customs (such as handwashing at meals, 15:2, phylacteries and tassels, 23:5, burial customs, 23:27); not to mention "an almost obsessive interest in and subtlety in the use of the Old Testament." But it is not just these details, as the "whole tone" of Matthew is set to present Jesus in terms a Jewish person would understand, "however radical and objectionable he might have found some aspects of its teaching" (1989, 97). Matthew is invested in Judaism, but has his own take on what that means, and what the "correct" way of being Jewish consists of.

In his discussion of whether Matthew's church was "inside" or "outside" of Judaism, France notes that real life is rarely as clear cut or straightforward as some scholarly scenarios might suggest. He finds the entire debate unsatisfactory and argues that for a Jewish person who chose to follow Jesus, there was an inevitable tension of being simultaneously "inside," in the sense of self-identifying as Jewish, but also "outside," in the sense of offering "a fierce repudiation of official non-Christian Judaism" (1989, 101).

France's recognition of the mess of real life is a helpful corrective to an overly neat and tidy theoretical academic proposal. Perhaps the best response to the question of the relationship between Matthew and Judaism is to argue that Matthew's community was in a liminal space, and this produced tension and fear, some of which manifests itself in the text of the Gospel. But can we be certain that it was written for a single community?

Matthew for all Christians?

There is an established trend within New Testament studies of reconstructing specific communities as the primary target audiences of each of the four Gospels. The challenge of this approach is that it is speculative, hypothetical and in danger of circular arguments. Not all scholars agree that the Gospels should be understood in this way, and I close this chapter with an overview of the counter-arguments.

Richard Bauckham's primary focus is to recover the idea that the Gospels are eyewitness testimony rather than veiled accounts of the communities for which they were allegedly written (2017, 4). He adds that the Gospels "were written within living memory of the events they recount" (2017, 7). Bauckham's main point is that the notion of a "Matthean Community" (or for that matter a "community" associated with any of the four gospels) is in fact a modern invention that has little substantive impact on the formation of the canonical texts. In Bauckham's reconstruction, the model was not of communal transmission of testimony, but of one named individual passing testimony on to another named individual. He supports this suggestion by explaining that this was the model that second century Christian writers used when describing their forebears (2017, 34-35).

Although Bauckham's focus is on eyewitness testimony, he concedes the case is more complex for the First Gospel. He notes that there is no direct reference, or even allusion to, eyewitness testimony in Matthew. This stands in marked contrast to the role of Peter in Mark, the Beloved Disciple in John, and Luke's various eyewitnesses. Indeed, whilst Matthew is present when Jesus speaks his final words (28:16-17), he is not singled out and isn't even called until chapter nine, by which time lots has happened. Bauckham concludes that "in general this Gospel, unlike the others, seems not concerned to claim the authority of any specific eyewitnesses" (2017, 131-32). This is interesting to reflect upon, especially when engaging with the scholars whose work is discussed in detail above. If those who argue for a Galilean, post-destruction of the Temple, context, are right, then the claim to authority is less about individual eyewitnesses and more about proving the continuity with and fulfilment of the Law? Is the Torah the witness to Jesus in Matthew?

Bauckham's primary point is that far from hinting as the community as a whole as the source of the Gospels, the New Testament texts are in fact "full of prominent named individuals" (2017, 297). But Christianity is not simply an individualistic project; it has a clearly communal focus. So how did the community remember? Bauckham distinguishes between (1) social dimension of individual recollection (2) shared recollections of a group and (3) collective memory. To avoid an overly individualistic focus, note that it is "as members of the groups to which they belong that individuals remember even their personal recollections." Thus, groups of Christians who were not eyewitnesses were appropriating the memories of the eyewitnesses into their group (2017, 313-14).

The relevance for this study is that whilst it is tempting to reconstruct a hypothetical Matthean community and their opponents, in Antioch or Sepphoris, the most pressing task is to read the text as we have it, and to remember the interpretative strategy of most Christians, which is to take the text at face value and presume it is an account of what Jesus said and did, not a reflection of an argument between Matthean Christ following Jews and other Jews about who Jesus is. Whilst readers of this book might come with an academic interest in the history and origin of the text, and recognise that Matthew's context will have influenced his approach, we must also acknowledge that not everyone brings this level of sophistication to their interpretation of the text. Bauckham's point is a helpful one, in reminding us of the danger of building hypothesis on presumption upon theory about the relationship between Matthew and his fellow Jews. Whilst we must make some attempts, we should also recognise any proposals are always provisional, and concentrate on the text as we have it and read it today. This is, I think, a compelling way of reading Matthew, and allows us to ask what he was trying to achieve by including "his blood be upon us," and contrasting that with the impact those words have, in fact, had on the generations that have read his text.

Conclusions

This chapter has discussed the date and place of composition of Matthew's Gospel, as well as the author's purpose in writing and the nature of the first audience(s) of the text. Personally, I am not completely persuaded by Carter's Rome-focused interpretation, although value it as a corrective to a solely Jerusalem and Judaism focused reading of Matthew. I remain largely agnostic on the place of composition, but find Gale's arguments reasonably persuasive. I concur with Nolland and Quarles that there is nothing in the text which mandates composition after 70 CE, which I recognise makes Gale's reconstruction questionable in some senses. Similarly, Bauckham's "for all Christians" argument is useful to remind us that any reconstruction of Matthew's context is subjective and hypothetical. In terms of the argument of this book, the main points to note are that Matthew is a part of an intra-Jewish argument about the person and significance of Jesus of Nazareth. It is important to recognise that Matthew was part of a threatened minority community. This shaped his language and approach to telling the story of Jesus. Whilst we do not have access to his precise context, we can reconstruct enough to understand the basic details. France's point about the messiness of reality, and therefore the liminal space occupied by Matthew and his fellow followers of Jesus, is useful for building a picture of the context in which the Gospel was written. This is a sufficient grounding from which to begin the task of the next chapter, discussing what Matthew means when he says Jesus fulfils the law.

Chapter 2
Fulfilment of the Law

The focus of this chapter is a discussion of how Matthew understands the relationship between the Torah and Jesus. It is thus a way of examining how Matthew can be simultaneously pro-Jewish and anti-Jewish. In the first few chapters of his Gospel, Matthew has a number of direct quotations of the Hebrew Scriptures, which he says are fulfilled in Jesus. There are also numerous allusions to incidents, people and texts in the Hebrew Scriptures, especially to the Prophet Isaiah. In 5:17, Jesus says "Do not think that I have come to abolish the law or the prophets; I have come not to abolish but to fulfil." What did all of this mean for Matthew and his community of Jewish followers of Jesus? What does it mean for us today? This chapter will explore those two questions, primarily through a discussion of 5:17-20 in particular and the Sermon on the Mount in general. The chapter is divided into four parts. First, some brief words of caution at the start. Second, an overview of how six scholars who are broadly in the "Matthew within Judaism" school reconstruct the original context of the Sermon on the Mount. Third, an exploration of six modern evangelical commentators' views. As noted above, these two groups were selected for their interest in responding to the final form of the text; their different concerns about the relationship with first-century Judaism and the topicality of their responses. Fourth, conclusions, particularly lessons for contemporary followers of Jesus. The main argument of this chapter is that Matthew sees Jesus as embodying the purpose and intended goal of the Torah, which means all future relationships with the divine should be conducted through him.

Beaton (2002, 17-34) surveys research into Matthew's use of the Old Testament. He notes there are forty explicit citations, twenty-one implicit quotations and "numerous allusory references" (2002, 17). This leads Beaton to conclude that fulfilment is "one of the great assumptions of the Matthean narrative," as Matthew demonstrates the "continuity of God's purposes in the life and ministry of Jesus of Nazareth with the history of the Jewish people" (2002, 18). Some of Matthew's references to the Hebrew Scriptures are particular to him; other elements are common to the other synoptics. Scholarship has tended to focus on the unique elements, perhaps to the detriment of a holistic understanding of how the Hebrew Scriptures are foundational to Matthew's account of Jesus' life. Matthew's "formula quotations" serve his "programmatic development of the theme of Jesus' fulfilment of the will of God" (2002, 23). Matthew's Gospel is simultaneously pro- and anti-Jewish, or perhaps can be understood as appropriating Jewish history and theology whilst propagating a radically new understanding of future relationship with God.

The need for caution in interpretation

In any dialogue what you say is less important than how you are heard. In her discussion of whether the Synoptic Gospels present good news or bad news, Amy-Jill Levine gives an example of how the same text can be heard in different ways. Citing Jesus asking "Why are you concerned about what you eat or what you wear?" she explains that if this is read in an interfaith gathering, it sounds like a criticism of Jews – and others – who demonstrate their faith through their dietary and clothing choices. She warns also of the danger of Christians reading the positive parts of the Old Testament as about them and the negative parts as about Jews only (2002, 77-78). This is an important point to bear in mind in a chapter focused on Matthew's fulfilment theology. I will concentrate on Matthew 5:17-20, but where appropriate make reference to other texts within the First Gospel. But before discussing the texts in detail, some words of caution from two Jewish scholars regarding how to interpret the Sermon on the Mount.

Levine and Brettler argue that antithesis is an unhelpful label for Matthew 5:21-47, since an antithesis implies opposition, and Jesus is not opposing the Torah. They jokingly suggest that a true antithesis would be

> "You have heard it said to those in ancient times, 'You shall not murder' and 'whoever murders shall be liable to judgement'" (Matt 5:21) – "But I say to you, lock and load!" (2020, 182).

They explain that we should not understand 5:21-47 as a rejection of Old Testament Torah in favour of New Testament love and mercy. Rather, Matthew's concern is to present Jesus as the new Moses. The aim is not to abrogate, but to extend the stipulations of Torah. For Matthew, "fulfil" doesn't mean "Jesus does what needs to be done so you don't have to" but "complete" in the "sense of drawing out the full implications of Torah and the Prophets." Jesus sets a high standard of ethical behaviour which he expects his followers to adhere to (2020, 182-84).

In an earlier work, Levine argues that the only actual "antithesis" of this section of the Sermon on the Mount is Matthew 5:43-44: "You have heard that it was said, 'You shall love your neighbour and hate your enemy.' But I say to you, love your enemies and pray for those who persecute you." She argues that no law commands hatred of enemies. On the contrary, Proverbs 25:21 advises, "If your enemies are hungry, give them bread to eat, and if they are thirsty, give them water to drink." Granted, there is a compensatory aspect to this bit of wisdom, for the proverb does indicate that those who do behave in such a beneficent manner toward enemies "will heap coals of fire on their heads, and the Lord will reward you" (Proverbs 25:22). Jesus therefore goes a step beyond the biblical tradition. Nevertheless, at least the enemy gets fed, and it might be a good reminder to those who hear his words in the Sermon on the Mount that "loving the enemy" also involves physical care, including "daily bread" (Levine 2006, 47).

Sadly, generations of Christians have been taught to read the Sermon on the Mount as a blanket condemnation of "the Jews." As Levine comments

> Church homilies and sermons, daily and weekly Bible study, and even respected academic monographs depict, both explicitly and implicitly, a Judaism that is monolithic, mired in legal minutiae, without spiritual depth, and otherwise everything that (they hope) Christianity is not (2006, 119).

This is a wholly inaccurate portrayal of Judaism that must be rejected out of hand. Yet many Christians are not even aware that these views are problematic. It is fairly common to hear the "Pharisee" being used as a synonym for "dry legalist with no real relationship with God." Many preachers and teachers (including those educating children and young people in the Christian faith) operate from a simplistic binary of all Jews were obsessed legalists with no real relationship with God whilst all Christians have a vibrant, living relationship with God through Jesus. This (unconscious) bias is one that Christian readers of this discussion would benefit from being aware of as they consider the argument developed below. What do Christians mean when they say that Jesus "fulfils the law"?

Matthew within Judaism

The concern to read Matthew within Judaism is reflected in the views of at least six recent scholarly discussions of the passage that is the focus of discussion here. These are offered as a representative sample of a recent move within academic New Testament studies to interpret Matthew's Gospel as primarily a Jewish text. As noted above, this is not an entirely problem-free approach. But it is nevertheless a helpful corrective to the fallacy that Jesus dispenses with Judaism in its entirety. The six scholars discussed are Anthony Saldarini, John Kampen, J Andrew Overman, James Crossley, Jordan Ryan, and Aaron Gale.

Anthony Saldarini

First, Saldarini's exploration of "Matthew's Torah" argues that far from superseding Jewish law by introducing a new Christian law or annulling it by focusing on the spirit of the law, in Matthew's Gospel, Jesus is established as the authoritative teacher of the law. Saldarini argues that in the first-century, interpretation of the law was primarily a political activity, focused on societal control; those whose understanding of the law became dominant were able to shape society according to their views. Matthew's views on the law are therefore part of his wider work to legitimise his own group in the ongoing conflict with the religious authorities of his day.

Saldarini surveys six topics: Sabbath laws; purity and dietary laws; tithes and taxes; divorce; oaths and vows; and circumcision. He notes that there is no mention of the final topic in Matthew, arguing that this indicates it was not controversial for the Matthean group as it was for Paul. Saldarini suggests two understandings of how the law is fulfilled: first, in Jesus' life, "which corresponds to God's promises in the Bible," and second in Jesus' teachings, "which lay bare the true meaning and requirements of the law" (1994, 161). Fulfilment is not about replacement of the law with Jesus or abrogation of the law by the love command, but rather a dynamic process of interpretation and obedience. The Ten Commandments are argued to be more fundamental than the purity laws (15:17-19), bind over against sectarian traditions (15:3-6, 20) and the foundation of Jesus' particular emphases (5:21-30). The other key qualities Matthew emphasises are justice, mercy, faithfulness, and Godlike perfection. These take precedence over the Sabbath in response to human need (12:1-4), over tithing (23:23-24) and give sinners access to Jesus (9:9-13). There is a transformation of human relationships, based on Jesus' greater justice, so that divorce, oaths and legal retaliation will become unnecessary (5:20-42). This is all summarised in the two great commandments (22:34-40), focused on living in the ideal community, which is ruled over by God, that is, the kingdom of heaven (1994, 124-64). This raises an interesting question: is Matthew primarily a political or a polemical document? Chapter one noted Warren Carter's argument that the Gospel is primarily a challenge to the (religious and political) might of Imperial Rome. The distinction between political and religious life is a modern one that did not apply in the first century CE. Nevertheless, it is worth recognising that Matthew is not simply making polemical points; he is making claims that apply to the entirety of his readers' lives, including who their ultimate master is.

John Kampen

Second, Kampen argues that the Sermon on the Mount should be read as a polemical text. He argues that there is plenty of evidence which documents the variety of discussions and disagreements between first-century Jews in Galilee and Judea about how to interpret the Torah and fulfil its requirements. For Kampen, Matthew's Gospel in general, and the Sermon on the Mount in particular, is one particular Jewish understanding of the law and argument as to how those requirements are to be fulfilled (2019, 68). Kampen also concurs with many other scholars in arguing that Matthew develops a typology of Jesus as the new Moses over the first four chapters of his gospel, and that this is the context for the teaching which begins in chapter five (2019, 73).

Kampen begins his discussion of Jesus and the law by noting that the Judaism of Jesus' day had no creeds. The boundaries of ancient Jewish communities, he observes, were set not by belief, but by practice. Kampen proposes that 5:17-20 set out the legal principles of interpretation adopted by Matthew's community, and that 5:21-48 illustrate the implications and method of this legal practice. He explains that Matthew puts Jesus at the centre of an ongoing first-century discourse amongst Jews about Moses and how to interpret the Torah he received; Jesus takes his audience back to Sinai to hear with Moses the law as received from God. The twist is that Jesus is now the definitive interpreter of that law. Thus, "the way that Jesus taught is the only manner in which it [the law] can be fully kept or observed" (2019, 90). This point is underlined by reference to "righteousness." It has already been established at his baptism that Jesus came to fulfil all righteousness (3:15); now the point is driven home through a focus on the law and how to obey it (2019, 85-92). Whilst twenty-first century Protestant Christians may think primarily in terms of orthodoxy, and be concerned about what people say and believe, Matthew and his contemporaries were much more interested in orthopraxy, that is, in appropriate, orthodox, behaviour. This is a helpful corrective and counter to any charges of Jewish legalism.

J. Andrew Overman

Third, Overman is clear that Matthew 5:17 does demand obedience to the Torah, indeed he proposes that adherence to the commandments was a natural presumption of any pious Jew of the day. The fact that Matthew has Jesus say this is indicative, in Overman's reading, of the controversy between the Matthean community and its opponents, who accuse them of playing fast and loose with the law. Overman proposes that Matthew was concerned that the charge was having an impact; maybe those younger in the faith were being convinced by the arguments of Matthew's opponents. He wonders whether families were becoming divided over the issue. And this was a serious debate, not merely about arcane prohibitions, but concerned with personal and corporate identity. The law was the boundary marker for Jewish identity, so failure to adhere to it was a failure to be Jewish (1996, 77-80). If Overman's reconstruction is correct, then the main purpose of the Sermon on the Mount is to persuade the Matthean followers of Jesus that they had made the right choice and should remain faithful in following Jesus.

James Crossley

Fourth, Crossley argues that "Matthew stressed, in some way, the ongoing validity of the Torah, at least for Jesus and probably for Jewish followers in the movement too" (2020, 30). Crossley explains that in Matthew Jesus is typically presented as conservative on matters of Torah interpretation, and as the comment in 5:17 makes clear, Jesus intends to fulfil, not abolish, the Torah. Crossley examines the so-called antitheses in detail, arguing they are not antithetical, in that they do not oppose the Torah; rather they clarify the intention behind the law. Similarly, the debates about the correct interpretation of the instruction to keep sabbath, to tithe and maintain purity present Jesus as a conservative exegete. This suggests Matthew was not only in favour of ongoing Torah observance, but also that he was familiar with the technicalities of the debates. Crossley concludes that whilst Matthew appears to hold with continued Torah observance for Jewish people, including Jewish disciples of Jesus, the text is silent as to the expectation placed on gentiles, which may well mean Matthew believed them to be exempt. This position is supported, Crossley believes, by the lack of any reference to circumcision. The commands of Matthew 5, especially in relation to reducing violence or sexual immorality, set a basic standard that all are expected to follow.

Jordan Ryan

Fifth, Ryan's argument focuses on exploring the relationship between Matthew 4:23, which states that Jesus taught in synagogues throughout Galilee, and the Sermon on the Mount. Ryan is not arguing this sermon was delivered in a synagogue, but rather that its tone and style is reflective of the teaching that Jesus undertook in the synagogues of Galilee. He proposes that "In the Sermon on the Mount, Matthew has constructed what we might call an eschatological synagogue, an assembly not of a local community but of the regathered people of God" (2020, 54). This may, perhaps, indicate a focus beyond a Jewish audience.

Ryan discusses what is known about synagogues in the first century CE, noting two competing theories, first that they functioned in a fashion similar to Greco-Roman associations and second that they acted more like public municipal institutions. Ryan suggests both types of synagogue existed, favouring the latter option in relation to those synagogues where Jesus taught. A further point of orientation is the reality that Matthew has shaped the structure and focus of chapters five to seven. That is not to say Jesus did not teach what is recorded here, but rather to recognise the setting of it all being delivered in a single sermon is an artificial creation of the author. Ryan argues that the concluding remarks (7:29) indicate the audience contrasting what they have just heard with a typical scribal synagogue teaching; that the teaching itself is indeed typical of that given in synagogues but that the main focus was not on a local gathering but on the reformed people of God. This pushes the reconstructed hypothetical Matthean community in the direction of Bauckham's "Matthew for all Christians" position. The reminder that Jesus did not just teach Jewish people builds on Crossley's argument.

Aaron Gale

Sixth, writing in the Jewish Annotated New Testament, Gale argues that the antitheses of 5:21-48 are an intensification of the demands of the Torah; they can be seen to "build a fence" around the law (see *m. Avot* 1.1), that is they "mandate observing a law well beyond its minimum requirements to ensure that the law itself is observed" (2017, 18). This is because in Matthew Jesus upholds the Torah (2017, 20).

From this brief overview, it is evident that those who hold to the Matthew within Judaism school of interpretation are clear that Jesus was a Torah-observant Jew, who expected (in Matthew's version of events) that his (Jewish) followers would do the same. Fulfilment of the law does not mean abrogation or nullification of the law. The commands of the Torah must still be obeyed by those Jews who have put their faith in Jesus. The Matthew within Judaism school's reconstruction of the context in which Matthew writes indicates primarily an internal struggle within Judaism to determine whose interpretation of the law is definitive, and whose teaching authority is final. These scholars do not focus on the implications for subsequent generations; in what follows, the views of six contemporary evangelical commentators are explored to give an indication of how modern (gentile) followers of Jesus are being taught to respond to these same texts.

Six evangelical views

In what follows, I will discuss the views of six evangelical scholars to indicate how those who hold a conversion-orientated faith treat the topic of fulfilment and Torah obedience, as well as their views on the implications for followers of Jesus today. The six who are discussed are R T France, Donald Hagner, Craig Keener, John Nolland, Tom Wright and Martin Goldsmith.

R T France

In his overview of Matthew's theology, France discusses the topic of "fulfilment" at length, arguing it is the central theme of Matthew's Gospel. France suggests that the prologue to the Gospel (1:1-2:23) is a manifesto as to how Jesus fulfils the Old Testament. The use of quotations from and allusions to the Hebrew scriptures throughout Matthew further emphasise this point, with the ten quotations beginning with "that it might be fulfilled…" (1:22-23; 2:15; 2:17-18; 2:23; 4:14-16; 8:17; 12:17-21; 13:35; 21:4-5;

27:9-10) being a particularly obvious case in point. Matthew also makes numerous typological references to the Hebrew scriptures, depicting Jesus as the new Moses and as "something greater" than the temple, or Jonah, or Solomon. When he discusses Jesus' relationship with and teaching about the Torah, France argues that the law is to remain authoritative, but it functions in a new way. He explains that in the law, "the focus of God's purpose is now to be found in Jesus rather than in the Old Testament in its own right" (1989, 196). The law remains a revelation of divine will, but must now be interpreted in the light of Jesus' life, death and resurrection. Jesus therefore functions as the turning-point of history, bringing in the new era in which the kingdom of heaven has drawn near (1989, 166-205).

France explores the teaching about Israel within Matthew's Gospel, arguing that it implies the whole people of God somehow finds their fulfilment in Jesus and the community that have gathered to follow him. France notes examples of typology where Jesus fulfils the role of Israel, with particular emphasis being given to Jesus as the Isaianic servant of the Lord (8:17; 12:17-21) and the Danielic Son of Man (10:23; 16:27-28; 24:30, 34; 26:64). But at the same time there are also typological references linking Israel and the church, notably the use of the Greek term *ekklesia* (16:18; 18:17), which elsewhere is the standard translation of the Hebrew *qahal*, the "congregation" of God's people. In Matthew, Jesus also speaks of judgement on the temple and on "this generation" for their failure to believe in him (see 21:33 for example) (1989, 206-18).

In his more recent commentary, France argues that if 5:17-20 are read in isolation, then they give the impression that Matthew presumes a Christian disciple must fully obey all the demands of the Torah. But this is at odds not simply with the rest of the New Testament, but even with the argument of the Gospel of Matthew itself (see especially 15:11). France suggests that the sayings in 5:17-20 may have been made on different occasions, but are gathered here to make a coherent point about Jesus' attitude towards the law, in part as a response to accusations circulating in Matthew's day that Jesus had set himself up against the written word of God. France concentrates on the meaning of "fulfil," proposing it is less about Jesus' particular actions or teaching in relation to the law, and more about the way in which Jesus fulfils the pattern of the law and the prophets; Jesus' life and ministry are understood as the culmination of that to which the law and the prophets pointed (2007, 178-184). France's position could be understood as advocating a supersessionist understanding of Judaism. France himself does not make this claim, but his point about culmination indicates the Torah is now of limited relevance for relationship with God. Those who follow this line of thought must consider the wider implications that follow.

Donald Hagner

Second, Donald Hagner argues that the ethical teaching of Jesus that is found in the Sermon on the Mount, as well as elsewhere in the Gospel, "has such a radical character and goes so much against what was the commonly accepted understanding of the commands of the Torah that it is necessary at the outset to indicate Jesus' full and unswerving loyalty to the law" (1993, 103). Hagner discusses the meaning of "fulfil" in 5:17 at length, contrasting different options. The possibilities that Hagner outlines are: (1) "to do or obey" the commandments of the Hebrew Scriptures; (2) a reference to Jesus' life and/or what is achieved by his death and resurrection; (3) teaching about the law so as to (a) "establish" or "uphold" the law or (b) add to and therefore "complete" the law or (c) "bring out the intended meaning of the law through definitive interpretation." Hagner suggests this means the reference is either to Jesus' words, his actions, or both. He rejects option one because Matthew never uses "fulfil" in the sense of obedience elsewhere in the gospel. The second option is also discarded, primarily because it does not fit the context. This leaves the third, which Hagner proposes should be understood not in the sense of establishing or adding to the law, but rather "bringing it to its intended meaning in connection with the messianic fulfilment" that has been brought about by Jesus (1993, 105-6). Thus, for Hagner, Jesus fulfils the Jewish messianic hope. Hagner's claims for the distinction between Jesus' teaching and that of his contemporaries are perhaps exaggerated. While there clearly are differences of opinion, they are more about who Jesus is than the ethics that he taught and practised.

Craig Keener

Third, in his discussion of 5:17-20, Keener begins by explaining that Jesus expected total obedience to the Jewish scriptures. He makes four main points. First, that Jesus affirms his commitment to the Torah. Thus "fulfil" is understood in the sense of teaching in accordance with it and "confirming" it by obedience. Second, Jesus utilises a popular rabbinic teaching on the immutability of the law to emphasise his point. Keener argues that reference to the "smallest letter" indicates the Hebrew letter *yodh*,

> which Jewish teachers said would not pass from the law. They said that when Sarai's name was changed to Sarah, the *yodh* removed from her name cried out from one generation to another, protesting its removal from Scripture, until finally, when Moses changed Oshea's name to Joshua, the *yodh* returned to Scripture (1999, 178).

Thus, in Keener's understanding of this teaching, the law will remain unchanged until the Kingdom of Heaven is fully consummated.

The accuracy of this argument is debatable; the quotation is from Bereshit Raba 47:1, which is attributed to Shimon Bar Yochai who lived in the second century CE. The text reads as follows:

> God said..., 'Sarai your wife...'" In Proverbs (12:4), it is written, "A woman of valor is a crown to her husband." Rabbi Aha said, "Her husband was crowned through her, but she was not crowned through her husband." Our rabbis taught that she ruled over her husband. In all places, the man gives orders, but here (Genesis 21:12), "In all that Sarah orders you, listen to her voice." Said Rabbi Yehoshua Ben Korcha: "The Yodh that the Holy One of Blessing took from Sarai was given half to Sarah, and half to Avraham. Said Rabbi Shime'on Bar Yochai: The Yodh that the Holy One of Blessing took from Sarai flew and posted itself in front of the Throne of the Holy One, and said: "Master of the Universe! Because I am the smallest letter You took me out of the name of Sarai the Righteous!" The Holy One said: "In the past you were in the name of a woman, and in the

end of the name! Now I will put you in the name of a man, and on the beginning of the name, as it is written 'And Moshe called Hosea Bin Nun Yehoshua'" (Numbers 13:16). Said Rabbi Mana: Sarai was just [a princess] for herself, now she will be a princess for all the world. (Bereshit Rabah 47:1, taken from sefaria.org, Sefaria community translation).

It is hard to see how this text can be read as teaching something about not changing the Torah. Rather, the midrashic context is about gender relations. There is no real link with Jesus' comments in Matthew 5. Although God does change Sarai's name to Sarah, that takes place within the Genesis narrative. It is true that Genesis is part of the Torah, but it's not part of the Torah in the legal sense meant here. Torah is assumed to be an authentic record of divine revelation, and there is no contemporaneous discussion of prohibition against changing the law.

Third, Keener argues Jesus says that people will be judged according to their response to God's Word. Fourth, one cannot pick and choose which commandments to obey, but must conform to them all (1999, 177-79). Keener thus sees Jesus' teaching as more in conformity with his contemporaries than Hagner does. Aside from his unpersuasive second point, the other three suggestions do develop a rounded understanding of what Matthew understood "fulfil" to mean.

John Nolland

Fourth, Nolland argues that Matthew's Gospel is written about the Jewish people; in Nolland's understanding, Matthew expects Jewish attitudes towards Jesus to change. Although he was initially rejected by the Jewish people, in time they will, Matthew hopes, welcome him. The mission to the gentiles is also a mission to the Jews; the Matthean Christians are not to cut off all contact with Jewish people nor are they to forget their roots. In a long footnote, Nolland also discusses Bauckham's thesis that the four canonical Gospels were all written as open documents, not for any particular community. Whilst he welcomes the corrective of this thesis, agreeing with Bauckham that an overly detailed attempt at reconstructing the Matthean community is a flawed exercise, Nolland is also clear that Matthew (and the other Gospel writers) did, both consciously and unconsciously, have particular groups of people in mind when they wrote (2005, 17-18).

Nolland discusses Matthew's use of the Old Testament in some detail, and concludes that there are eight ways in which he does so. First, Matthew sometimes retells Old Testament stories to provide context for the coming of Jesus. Second, to claim fulfilment of a previously unfulfilled prophecy, and third, the related category of claiming eschatological fulfilment of a partially fulfilled prophecy. Fourth, identifying biblical patterns that are related to Jesus. Fifth, indicating fundamental ethical principles. Sixth, providing paradigms from the history of God's people that seem relevant to the context of Jesus. Seventh, appealing to an element of an ideal future in order to criticise the present. Eighth, "to locate a foundation in a divine self-declaration for arguing a particular view" (2005, 36). Nolland is also clear that Matthew made use of other Jewish material, citing for example the haggadic traditions of Moses' infancy as being relevant to the accounts of Jesus' infancy in 1:18-25 (2005, 37).

In describing Matthew's theology, Nolland states that he writes "out of and into a Jewish context," and does so on the basis of Jewish presuppositions about the nature of God (2005, 38). Yet he brings his own perspective, that in Jesus, the God of Israel is doing a new thing, bringing about the arrival of the kingdom of heaven. Thus, Jesus reveals "the full intention of the Mosaic Law," and is the only reliable guide as to this new way of living, which he himself lives out fully. Ultimate loyalty is therefore primarily to him. Jesus is a lightning rod for divine judgement and justice. This does not mean no other judgement will fall on anyone; the eventual destruction of Jerusalem and the temple makes that point plain. Rather it means that those who align themselves wholeheartedly with Jesus will be spared the judgement that would otherwise be rightfully theirs (2005, 39-41).

Turning to the Sermon on the Mount, Nolland argues that

As radical as its demands are, this is no manual for an exclusive spiritual elite. Its concern to elucidate the will of God is based on theological and ethical considerations and is not linked to a distinctive call for an exclusive few (2005, 192).

For Nolland, the Sermon on the Mount is thus addressed widely to both followers of Jesus and also to those who are merely curious about his teaching. Nolland recognises that there was doubtless a strand of Jewish anti-Christian polemic that sought to dismiss Christianity as an upstart religion which sought to overturn their ancestral Mosaic Law. Thus, Jesus may also be responding to this possible critique by saying he comes to fulfil not destroy the law.

Nolland discusses what "fulfil" might mean in some detail, rejecting ideas of addition to the law, replacement of the old law with a new law or a spirit of love that transcends, and of perfectly living out the requirements of the law. In Nolland's view, the language of fulfilment indicates "a claim that Jesus' programmatic commitment, far from undercutting the role of the Law and Prophets, is to enable God's people to live out the Law more effectively," in part through providing deeper insights into the true meaning of the Law, which undercut the superficiality of much interpretation (2005, 218-19). Thus, for Nolland, Jesus demands total obedience. What price those who reject him?

Tom Wright

Fifth, for Tom Wright, Matthew's Gospel is not setting up a new Israel, but rather casting the followers of Jesus as the true descendants of Abraham, Isaac and Jacob. This is seen in the so-called "fulfilment" passages (1:22; 2:5, 15, 17, 23 etc), but is in fact part of the entire plot of the Gospel, which presumes the whole story of the Jewish people to date. Jesus (the Greek translation of "Joshua") is, in fact, the true heir to Moses, but he is more than this; he is Emmanuel, Israel's God "coming to be with his people as they emerge from their long exile, remaining with them still as they go on to possess the land" (1:23; 28:20, Wright 1993, 389). Thus, Matthew is a biography of Jesus, but it is much more than this; it is "the continuation and climax of the story of Israel," which is in fact part of the story of the whole world. In telling this story, Wright concludes Matthew is undoubtedly subverting the Jewish worldview of his time as he retells Israel's story in the light of Jesus (1993, 390).

In his popular *For Everyone…* commentary series, Wright does not discuss the theology of Matthew in detail, but rather makes some more general observations. When he explores 5:13-20, Wright suggests Jesus was both faithful and revolutionary. Wright explains that Jesus "was indeed offering something utterly revolutionary, to which he would remain faithful; but it was, in fact, the reality towards which Israel's whole life and tradition had pointed" (2002a, 39-40). Wright reads the Sermon on the Mount first as a call to Israel to fulfil the calling God has placed on the nation, but secondly as a call to all new followers of Jesus – that is, all Christians – to do the same. He adds:

> Jesus wasn't intending to abandon the law and the prophets. Israel's whole story, commands, promises and all, was going to come true in him. But, now that he was here, a way was opening up for Israel – and through that, all the world – to make God's covenant a reality in their own selves, changing behaviour not just by teaching but by a change of heart and mind itself" (2002a, 41).

Wright's reading of fulfilment is thus that for Matthew, Jesus is the climax of the story of God's dealing with Israel. Through Jesus, the offer of entry into the covenant with the God of Israel is extended to all people, who are invited into a personal relationship with God in and through the person of Jesus. Wright's conclusions are thus similar to Nolland's. Jesus' teaching is to be obeyed completely; what will happen to those who reject it?

Martin Goldsmith

Finally, the Jewish convert to Christianity Martin Goldsmith has written a short commentary on Matthew, focused primarily on the implications for Christian mission and outreach. Goldsmith describes his early Christian experience as being predominantly gentile. Although he is of Jewish heritage, he became a Christian in response to the witness of a gentile, attended a largely gentile church, and trained to become a missionary in a gentile college. It was only when he lived and worked as a missionary in Northern Sumatra, Indonesia, that he began to think about the relationship between his own Jewish heritage and his Christian faith. Goldsmith says this was largely as a result of the more corporate and communal focus of the people he lived and worked amongst and that he "began a long pilgrimage of attempting to see the Bible and theology through my own Jewish eyes" (2001, vii-viii).

Several times throughout his book, Goldsmith issues clear warnings against replacement theology, explaining that the Church is not Israel. Rather, in Goldsmith's view, Matthew is writing in the face of rejection and antagonism, to strengthen the "Jewish Church" in a context where most Jewish people reject the concept of Jesus as Messiah, and where "the kingdom of Heaven seemed to have failed." But this does not mean Matthew is writing out of narrow parochial concern; Goldsmith is clear that Matthew is written to "give a true account of the history of Jesus," as well as encouraging his fellow Jewish Christians, and also opening up the possibility of faith to the Gentiles (2001, xiv).

Goldsmith focuses his analysis on the missiological implications of the text. He is agnostic on the location of the Matthean community, but clear it is primarily Jewish in heritage, that is, made up of Jews who believe in Jesus as the Messiah. Goldsmith is also clear that whilst the horror of the Holocaust must never be forgotten, this does not mean evangelism towards Jewish people is out of bounds (he does not address the history of Christian antisemitism). Indeed, he argues that any study of Matthew's Gospel must presume it is still possible for Jewish people to become followers of Jesus, although it should be noted this is very different from actively encouraging Jewish people to follow Jesus. The focus of his study is first on developing a rounded understanding of the person of Jesus of Nazareth as presented in Matthew's Gospel, and second, on examining the reactions that different groups have towards Jesus. He hopes to provide particular encouragement to those who follow Jesus in a context where Christians are a persecuted minority, believing that a clear eschatological hope in Jesus' sovereignty over history is necessary in such circumstances (2001, xv-xviii).

Goldsmith argues that in the Sermon on the Mount, Jesus is "revealing his teaching authority as against that of the leaders of Israel at that time" (2001, 62). Thus, any criticisms are particularly against those leaders. Goldsmith adds that for

> Matthew and his Jesus-believing community too, the struggle was on between the leaders of Israel and themselves for the hearts and minds of the ordinary people of Israel. Indeed, there was even a wider competition to win over the Gentile world in the Roman empire, for their traditional religions were losing their hold (2001, 62).

Thus, the Sermon on the Mount is not abstract moral teaching, but a claim to teaching authority in a marketplace of religious possibilities. Goldsmith discusses the Sermon on the Mount under six themes: kingdom; righteousness; rewards; mission; teaching; and authority (2001, 63-78). He explains that the essence of the teaching about the kingdom of heaven is found in the Lord's prayer: bringing glory to the Father, surrendering to his will, trusting in his provision and protection, forgiving others, and recognising that God alone is worthy of worship. A Christian community is to demonstrate righteous living, based on a proper recognition of divine holiness, a morally impeccable way of living that characterises both individuals and the community as a whole. Goldsmith's discussion of rewards concentrates on the beatitudes (5:3-12) and the exhortation to not worry but trust in God's provision (6:25-34), understanding the teaching to be a reminder that God has all things under his sovereign control. Goldsmith argues that both individuals and congregations are obligated to missional outreach, and that Matthew's Gospel encourages mission to all nations, even if there are some negative statements about gentiles within the text. Jesus' teaching in the Sermon on the Mount is clear and direct. Goldsmith also argues that Jesus is contributing his own views on contested topics of his day, such as dietary and purity laws, divorce, the payment of taxes and tithes, and keeping the Sabbath. Matthew carefully omits any material that might suggest Jesus did not obey the Torah, since he believes Jesus has come not to abolish the Law and the Prophets, but to fulfil them (5:17). Not only does Matthew favourably contrast Jesus and his followers with the Jewish religious leaders of his day, he also says they are better than any false prophets (7:15-20). Goldsmith also discusses teaching on the quality of relationships that should characterise the community of believers, a spirit of love and forgiveness, concern and compassion for all. Finally, Jesus' teaches on his own authority, which means that for us reading the text today, we should "understand Matthew's Gospel as a historical treatise which demonstrates the absolute authority of Jesus in both his teaching and his deeds" (2001, 77).

Goldsmith's Jewish heritage means that of the six commentators discussed, he is the most sensitive to the implications of his teaching for Jewish people today. Yet he presumes evangelism amongst Jewish people is to be encouraged, and does not address the historic or contemporary issues this attitude raises. Goldsmith is clear in his rejection of replacement theology, but this still leaves us with a question. What happens to those who do not have faith in Jesus?

So what?

This chapter has discussed what it means to believe that Jesus fulfils the law. The Matthew within Judaism school of interpretation provides a helpful correction to the lazy stereotype of Jewish legalism that is all too often deployed within Christian teaching for people of all ages and stages of maturity in faith. As will be discussed in subsequent chapters, there is a significant need for education of those who have positions of teaching authority, to ensure that more nuanced, accurate and fair presentations of Judaism are given. For the Matthew within Judaism school, the Sermon on the Mount generally, and Matthew 5:17-20 in particular, establish Jesus' credentials as an orthodox teacher of the Jewish faith who advocates orthopraxy. That is to say, what Jesus teaches and how he lives are both in conformity with the Torah. Scholars in the Matthew within Judaism school argue interpret the text as both including Jesus within Judaism but also as establishing the boundaries of the community he gathered around himself.

The work of contemporary evangelical scholars is, in part, an indication of how this strand of Christianity might respond to the challenge of (unwitting) Christian antisemitism. It is not the case that (most) Christians are intentionally antisemitic, rather that they simply do not realise how their statements are heard. A belief that in Jesus the Torah is fulfilled can easily become a belief that therefore Judaism is redundant and so Jews are unnecessary, a position that can even slip into justification of genocide. Whilst that is an extreme view, and not at all that of any of the scholars discussed above, it can be the first step on such a slippery slope. The expositions of France, Hagner, Nolland, and Wright discussed above could all lend themselves to just such an interpretation. That is not to say any of these scholars are antisemites, or that they set out to teach anti-Judaism. Rather it is a warning that, at the very least, evangelical scholars must beware of an unconscious bias that denigrates Judaism, both ancient and modern, without good cause or clear supporting evidence. This point becomes plain when we discuss the portrayal of, and commentary on, those whom Jesus opposes in Matthew's Gospel, the topic to which I turn next.

Chapter 3
Polemic and Opponents

The focus of this chapter is on the nature of polemic in a first-century Jewish context, as well as on discussing what can be discerned from the text of Matthew about those whom Jesus and Matthew's community opposed. Subsequent chapters will examine Matthew 23 and 27:25, arguably the most polemical and destructive sections of the gospel, in greater detail, but before doing so, it is important to outline what polemic is and how it functions. Although the discussion centres on language and its impact, the real concern is about power relations. This is because the power that individuals and groups have determines the impact of their polemic. One can be vitriolic, but if one lacks the power to turn one's threats into reality, then one is merely speaking words. On the other hand, the polemic of the powerful can easily become the pretext for persecution. We must therefore focus not simply on what was said, but also on the impact of those words.

This chapter is divided into seven parts. First, a brief introduction to polemic as a genre. Second, some comments on polemic in the Hebrew Scriptures, and third, anti-Jewish polemic in the New Testament. Fourth, Overman's citations of other contemporaneous polemical texts. Fifth, Kampen's discussion of sectarian first-century Judaism. Sixth, I explore the question of whether classifying Matthew as "just polemic" is an adequate solution before finally reaching the conclusion that this is not a sufficiently robust response; further work is needed to respond to the antisemitic potential of Matthew's Gospel.

What is polemic?

Polemical writing aims to persuade through negative and powerful rhetoric. Although the focus appears to be external, that may be more a matter of appearance than substance. As Levine and Brettler explain:

The main goal of polemic is to persuade. In some cases, the invective is internal: it seeks to persuade those already in a community to adhere to a particular set of beliefs or practices and so helps to strengthen communal identity (2020, 55).

This may well be the purpose of the polemic within Matthew's Gospel. That is to say, it is not written to attack external opponents, but rather to remind the internal audience of why they have made what is, in Matthew's view at least, the correct choice. It is important to remember when considering the polemic within Matthew that it forms part of a wider debate. As Levine and Brettler put it:

Christianity emerged from Jewish practice and belief, and rabbinic Judaism took shape, in places, in competition with Christian claims. In this process of self-definition, each side directed polemic against the other (2020, 56).

The existence of polemic on all sides of this debate is an important corrective to the danger of presuming it was simply the followers of Jesus who were abusive towards those they disagreed with. Levine and Brettler acknowledge the existence of anti-Christian polemic within the Talmud, noting that most Jews do not read the entirety of the Talmud, any more than Christians read the entirety of Martin Luther or the Church Fathers, and so are unaware of the existence of the polemic within these texts (2020, 57). Part of the challenge, therefore, in interpreting Matthew 23; 27:25 is that whilst the polemic of the Jewish followers of Jesus against their opponents is preserved accessibly in the New Testament, the counter-polemic, of those first-century Jews who did not recognise that Jesus was the Messiah, has not been preserved.

Mary C Callaway on prophetic critique in the Hebrew Bible

For some scholars, the best place to begin discussing the polemic of the Christian scriptures is to examine the polemic of the Hebrew texts. The argument is, in essence, that the polemic of the New Testament is in continuity with the polemic of the Old. Christian scholar Mary Callaway is typical in this regard.

Callaway begins her discussion by noting that "As a national epic, Israel's story is surprisingly sparse in the language of self-glorification; it is a story told in the voice of a relentless critic rather than a proud heir" (1993, 21). She explains this is because it is a story of God's dealing with his people, not of the glory of Israel as a nation. As such, the Hebrew Scriptures are full of critical and polemical addresses towards the people of God.

Callaway discusses the "woe oracles" of the prophets, citing examples such as the colourful language of Isaiah 5:18 and the lists of woes and consequences of 5:8-25. She also gives examples of lawsuit motifs such as Micah 6:1-2. Other features are the use of animal imagery, depicting Israel as worse than the beasts (Jeremiah 8:6-7; Isaiah 1:3); the description of Israel's leaders as predatory (Zephaniah 3:3); and the metaphor of sexual infidelity (Isaiah 1:21-23; Jeremiah 2:23-24). Israel's leaders are described as drunken sots (Isaiah 28:7-8; 29:9-10) and there is extensive use of sarcasm (such as Amos 4:4-5). Callaway proposes that whilst this language was offensive, it was also expected of prophets, even if those in power resisted the critique, as occurred in the case of Jeremiah and Amos.

Turning to the content of the prophetic critique, Callaway argues that "Israel's habit of self-criticism and its willingness to tolerate the invective of the prophets were balanced by a strong sense of its security in the promises of YHWH" (1993, 30), even if that sense of security was, at times, ill-founded. A prophet's authority rested on the claim to being called, to being a bearer of the divine word. Fundamentally, a prophetic critique was a theological, not a sociological or political one. The prophet was one who communicated the pain that was present in the heart of God because of the rebellion of his covenant people. Prophets both stood apart from the community to speak God's critique but at the same time they represented the people to God. She concludes that the picture of "bumbling Israel" allows the reader to see the truth of God's love and mercy dominating over justice and retribution. But there are dangers: first, that the recognition that the people continually fail to attain to God's standards leads to the inaccurate caricature of an Old Testament God of demands and vengeance. Second, and more seriously, there is a danger of Christians reading prophetic invective as historical description. "It is one thing for Jeremiah to call his own people stiff-necked; it is quite another for a Christian to refer to Jews that way" (1993, 38). Spoken by the Lord's chosen and called prophet, the rebuke led to life; spoken by an outsider, it was a precursor to abuse and death. Thus, context and identity of the speaker are crucial for interpretation of the text. Furthermore, one must ascertain whether the polemic is internally or externally focused. Hence it is important to consider the nature of polemic in more detail, the topic to which I now turn.

L T Johnson on the New Testament's "anti-Jewish slander"

Johnson's 1989 article on the New Testament's "anti-Jewish slander and the conventions of ancient polemic" has been utilised by many scholars as a way of contextualising some of the harsh language found within the New Testament. In the introduction to his article, Johnson explains what he is, and is not, setting out to do. In essence, his purpose is to examine the polemic of the New Testament to see what function this style of language serves. This is because:

> The power of such language to shape hostile and destructive attitudes and actions towards Jews has often been realized. The proper understanding of such polemic is therefore an issue of real importance (1989, 421).

Johnson initially surveys some ways of removing the problem. He rejects the possibility of censorship, arguing that there will be precious little left after a censor's scissors have got to work to exorcise all potentially offensive texts. Moreover, a text that one person finds offensive, might be positive, affirming and identity building for another person. It is not simply the case that everyone is in agreement that certain texts are entirely bad. A second strategy that Johnson rejects is that of historical vindication, namely arguing that the Jews did not kill Jesus, but the Romans. Johnson points out that solutions which seek to explain the problem away through presenting a more "accurate" understanding of history miss the point. It's all very well to say that the Pharisees were not all hypocrites nor were they all money loving. But that does not deal with the impact of the rhetoric. Third, he dismisses the concept of mistaken attribution, that Jesus was attacking not Jews generally, but specifically Pharisees of the house of Shammai, which means no reference is made to modern Judaism, which is arguably descended from the Pharisaic house of Hillel. (As will be discussed below, this reconstruction is of dubious accuracy; nevertheless, the point that Jesus is talking to a particular group of people, not Jews in general, remains of some limited explanatory value). In passing, he also notes the anachronism of referring to "Judaism" versus "Christianity" in the first century. Neither really existed at this point in time and so this is not useful either. For Johnson, none of these solutions are satisfactory, primarily because, it is not historical evidence, but rhetoric, that shapes the reader. Thus, his purpose in writing this argument is "not adjudicating the anti-Jewish slander of the NT, but showing how to understand it" (1989, 423). Johnson's approach here is useful; we must not ignore or try to explain away difficult passages; rather we must face up to them squarely and respond carefully.

Johnson first argues that the Jewish messianists (his term for the first followers of Jesus) were a tiny, powerless, insignificant minority, at most one hundred thousand compared to seven million Jews. It was the Jews who held all the power and status; before its destruction the Jerusalem temple was a wonder of the world, as were the synagogues of Sardis. Judaism had centuries of interaction with the world, a deserved reputation for antiquity and sophistication. By contrast the messianic movement centred on Jesus was a handful of years old, with no buildings, status or history of interaction with wider society. This means that New Testament rhetoric strives to make "a compensatory leap across the very real gap in power." As Johnson explains, when those speaking are relatively powerless, their abuse tends to become louder and more vitriolic. The second characteristic Johnson identifies is that New Testament rhetoric tends to be defensive, as the "symbols of Torah it had appropriated were so much more self-evidently in the control of the dominant group" Finally, what is particularly problematic is that once Christianity became politically more powerful than Judaism, the fear and hostility that had been shown when Christianity was weak continued to be displayed (1989, 424).

Johnson also references the diversity of the Messianic movement, and the contested and challenging period of internal debate over the precise identity and purpose of this new group. Concerned primarily with survival, these first followers of Jesus had no time or interest in the impact of their words on others. Johnson argues that the texts of the New Testament "clearly show that the need to secure identity was made more urgent because of the disagreements and disputes within the movement itself" (1989, 425). Thus, most of the polemic of the New Testament is inward facing, written to distinguish who are the "correct" members of the movement. His main example here is Paul; for example, Johnson argues that Galatians is not addressed towards Jews but against fellow followers of Jesus.

Moreover, first-century Judaism was thoroughly diverse; Johnson warns against falling for the founding myth of a unified Judaism birthed at Yavneh, as the reality was more complex. Indeed, some of the best evidence for diversity within first-century Judaism actually comes from the pages of the New Testament. Johnson concludes this part of his argument by explaining that when the New Testament was written

> neither Christianity nor Judaism had reached the point of uniformity and separation that would characterize them in later centuries. The messianists were part of a much larger debate within Judaism, a debate with many parties, concerning the right way to read Torah, the text that shaped the people (1989, 428).

This overview of the historical circumstances is a necessary but insufficient explanation; in Johnson's view, even if we know the context, the anti-Jewish polemic of the New Testament "still appears excessive" (1989, 428). For Johnson, polemic is best thought of as part and parcel of philosophical debate in that time. He proposes that the polemical rhetoric of the New Testament "is typical of that found among rival claimants to a philosophical tradition and is found as widely among Jews as among other Hellenists" (1989, 429). That is to say, first-century Judaism (including the first followers of Jesus) is best understood as competing philosophical schools of thought, and the rhetoric of the New Testament is simply how people talked to their opponents in that context.

Johnson develops his argument to explain that the purpose of slander is not factual but to distinguish who one's opponent was. "The purpose of the polemic is not so much the rebuttal of the opponent as the edification of one's own school. Polemic was primarily for internal consumption" (1989, 433). Johnson discusses Matthew 23 as a particular case in point. In his understanding, the focus is on the Matthean community. The text is an attack on rival teachers, with the purpose of providing positive instructions for the followers of Jesus in Matthew's community (23:8-11). Johnson also suggests there is a transitional function, from the public teaching of Jewish leaders in 22:15-26 to private instruction of Jesus' inner circle in chapter twenty-four.

Johnson gives examples of Jewish polemical rhetoric, especially from Hellenistic Jewish writings. One example is Josephus in "Against Apion." The text is Josephus' rebuttal to the accusations levelled by Apion against Jewish people in general. Josephus responds with similar polemic of his own, for example describing the Egyptians as "entirely of vain and foolish minds" (1:25) and personally attacking Apion, describing him as a "notorious liar" (2:2), an "author of sedition" (2:6), and asking rhetorically if Apion has "an ass's heart or the impudence of a dog" (2:7) (all quotes taken from sefaria.org).

Johnson notes that Philo is as rude at times:

> In *The Embassy to Gaius*, he more than reciprocates the Alexandrian hatred for Jews, calling them the "promiscuous and unstable rabble of the Alexandrians" (18.120). ... The Egyptians "are a seed bed of evil in whose souls both the venom and the temper of the native crocodiles and wasps are reproduced" (26.166) (1989, 435, translation from Colson 1971).

Johnson proposes that first-century Jews and Christians, in common with any people engaged in philosophical debate at that time, "simply do not hear the inflammatory nature of this language" (1989, 436). It was just the

way people talked to each other. Whilst this may be true, the point about
an imbalance of power relations, made above, must be borne in mind.

Johnson gives further examples of Josephus being negative about his
fellow. For example, "Josephus castigates the reviewer of his book *The
Jewish War*, Justus of Tiberias, as "a charlatan and a demagogue and a
deceiver" (*Life* 9 §40) (1989, 436, translation from Thackeray 1926).

Johnson concludes that when first-century Jews, which of course includes
the first followers of Jesus, engaged in debate with each other, they used
the polemical language, following the conventions and expectations of
their time. Johnson reiterates his point:

> If by definition sophists are hypocritical, and philosophers of all
> opposing schools are hypocritical, and philosophers in general are
> hypocritical, and Alexandrian pagans are hypocritical, and Apion is
> a hypocrite, are we really surprised to find scribes and Pharisees
> called hypocrites? If sophists are by definition blind, and Apion is
> blind, and Alexandrian pagans are blind, should we be shocked to
> see scribes and Pharisees called "blind guides" by Matthew? (1989,
> 440).

This is a valuable point. It is a necessary, but insufficient, explanation for
Christian teachers and preachers to draw attention to the stereotypical
nature of polemical language in first-century debate. The point could even
be made in the context of a church youth group, through reference, for
example, to the formulaic, stereotypical nature of playground insults.
Johnson's analysis is useful, but does not fully resolve the issue of how
Christians are to respond to the polemic found in Matthew.

Johnson offers four points in conclusion. First, reading the text in this way
makes the polemic more intelligible. Second, by the measure of
contemporary Jewish polemic, the New Testament's slander of fellow Jews
is comparatively mild. Johnson suggests there is harsher polemic against
gentiles (for example Matthew 6:7, 32; Romans 1:18-32) and deviant
members of the messianist movement (for example 2 Corinthians 11:1-6,
14-21; 2 Timothy 2:14-3:9). Third, the conventional nature of the polemic

means that it has a connotative not denotative function. That is, it indicates there are opponents rather than making specific charges against them, let alone describing them objectively. Fourth, all Jews, messianist and non-messianist used the conventions of Hellenistic rhetoric. As Johnson observes, "grasping the conventional nature of the polemic can rob such language of its mythic force and therefore its capacity for mischief" (1989, 441). This is a helpful first step in discerning how Christians can engage with some of the more challenging passages in Matthew; a necessary, but not sufficient, preliminary piece of exegesis. Christian teachers and preachers should bear this in mind during their preparatory work.

J. Andrew Overman on the polemic in Matthew

In Overman's reconstruction, Matthew's community were Jewish, and thought of themselves as the "true Israel," and "set themselves over against those they believed to be the false covenant people and false leaders who would lead the people astray" (1990, 5). Part of their response to this perception of reality was to write polemically about those they opposed. Like Johnson, Overman seeks to contextualise the polemic of Matthew through reference to other texts where polemical language is used against opponents (1990, 26-30).

First, Overman explains that 1 Enoch 104 "goes into considerable detail concerning the way in which sinners corrupt the Scriptures and the fact that the community of the righteous truly possesses the law and the true understanding of it" (1990, 26). There's more of the same throughout 1 Enoch 94-108; three examples will illustrate the point:

> Woe unto those who build oppression and injustice!
> Who lay foundations for deceit.
> They shall soon be demolished; and they shall have no peace.
> Woe unto those who build their houses with sin!
> For they shall all be demolished from their foundations;
> And they shall fall by the sword.
> Those who amass gold and silver; they shall quickly be destroyed.
> Woe unto you, O rich people!

For you have put your trust in your wealth.
You shall ooze out of your riches.
For you do not remember the Most High.
In the days of your affluence, you committed oppression.
You have become ready for death, and for the day of darkness and
the day of great judgement (1 Enoch 94:6-9, translated by Isaac 1983).

This denunciation begins in the third person but continues in a more direct address of condemnation of the rich for failing to honour God. The second text singles out the foolish for particular attack:

Woe unto you, fools, for you shall perish through your folly!
You do not listen to the wise, and you shall not receive good things.
And now do know that you are ready for the day of destruction.
Hope not that you shall live, you sinners, you who shall depart and
die,
For you know for what (reason) you have been ready for the day of
great judgement,
For the day of anguish and great shame for your spirits.
Woe unto you obstinate of heart, who do evil and devour blood!
From where (will you find) good things that you may eat, drink,
and be satisfied?
Even from all the good things which the Lord, the Most High,
stocked in plenitude upon the whole earth?
No peace exists for you!
Woe unto you who love unrighteousness!
Why do you have hopes for good things for yourselves?
Do know that you shall be given over into the hands of the
righteous ones,
And they shall cut off your necks and slay you, and they shall not
have compassion upon you.
Woe unto you who rejoice in the suffering of the righteous ones!
For no grave shall be dug for you.
Woe unto you who would set at nought the words of the righteous
ones!
For you shall have no hope in life.

Woe unto you who write down false words and words of
wickedness!
For they write down their lies so that they (the people) may commit
wicked acts,
And they cause others to commit wicked acts.
They shall have no peace, but shall die quickly (1 Enoch 98:9-16,
translated by Isaac 1983).

Third, an example of the woes within the text:

Woe unto you who cause wickedness!
Who glorify and honour false words,
You are lost, and you have no life of good things;
Woe unto you who alter the words of truth
And pervert the eternal law!
They reckon themselves not guilty of sin,
They shall be trampled on upon the earth (1 Enoch 99:1-2,
translated by Isaac 1983).

Overman presumably drew attention to these texts as a point of contrast
with the woes against the Pharisees found in Matthew 23. The reader may
find it helpful to read the passages one after the other and contemplate
which is harsher. From my own, albeit very brief analysis, the focus of the
Enoch texts is more on those who are identified as "wicked," whilst in
Matthew 23, Jesus is more focused on calling out what he sees as religious
hypocrisy.

There is also polemic in the Psalms of Solomon. Chapter four focuses on
the corrupt way in which the Jewish leadership have dealt with the law,
while chapter eight discusses violations in relation to the temple. The
righteous are those who obey the law, and they will inherit life as God
gathers a remnant of the faithful. Chapter four is reproduced below in full:

Why are you sitting in the council of the devout, you profaner?
And your heart is far from the Lord, provoking the God of Israel by
lawbreaking;

Excessive in words, excessive in appearance above everyone
He who is harsh in words in condemning sinners at judgement.

And his hand is the first one against him as if in zeal,
Yet he himself is guilty of a variety of sins and intemperance.
His eyes are on every woman indiscriminately,
His tongue lies when swearing a contract,
At night and in hiding he sins as if no one saw,
With his eyes he speaks to every woman of illicit affairs;
He is quick to enter graciously every house as though innocent.
May God remove from the devout those who live in hypocrisy;
May his flesh decay and his life be impoverished.
May God expose the deeds of those who try to impress people;
(and expose) their deeds with ridicule and contempt.
And the devout will prove their God's judgement to be right
When sinners are driven out from the presence of the righteous,
Those who please men, who deceitfully quote the Law.

And their eyes are on a man's peaceful house,
As a serpent destroys the wisdom of others with criminal words
His words are deceitful that (he) may accomplish (his) evil desires;
He did not stop until he succeeded in scattering (them) as orphans.
He devastated a house because of his criminal desire;
He deceived with words; (as if) there were no one to see and to judge.
He is satiated with lawless actions at one (place), and (then) his eyes are on another house
To destroy it with agitating words.
With all this his soul, like Hades, is not satisfied.

Lord, let his part be in disgrace before you;
May he go out groaning and return cursing.
Lord, may his life be in pain and poverty and anxiety;
May his sleep be painful and his awakening be anxious.
May sleep be taken away from his temples at night;
May he fail disgracefully in all the work of his hands.

May he return to his house empty-handed;
May his house lack everything; let it not satisfy his soul.
May his old age be in lonely childlessness until his removal.
May the flesh of those who try to impress people be scattered by
wild animals,
And the bones of the criminals (lie) dishonored out in the sun.
Let crows peck out the eyes of the hypocrites,
For they disgracefully empty many people's houses
And greedily scatter (them).
They have not remembered God,
Nor have they feared God in all these things;
But they have angered God, and provoked him.
May he banish them from the earth,
For they defrauded innocent people by pretense.

Blessed are those who fear God in their innocence;
The Lord shall save them from deceitful and sinful people
And save us from every evil snare.
May God banish those who arrogantly commit all (kinds of)
unrighteousness,
For the Lord our God is a great and powerful judge in
righteousness
Lord, let your mercy be upon all those who love you. (Translated
by Wright, 1985).

Perhaps there is a closer parallel in this text to Matthew 23. Certainly, the target is closer; both texts focus on corruption and failure of religious leadership. The tone of Psalms of Solomon appears, to me at least, to be at least as harsh, if not harsher than that found in Matthew.

In 2 Baruch, a late first-century document, it is personal attitude to the law that is "the determining factor in guaranteeing salvation or punishment in the coming age." God's law is life and is "virtually synonymous with wisdom and understanding" (Overman 1990, 27). A few examples are given below:

You, however, if you prepare your minds to sow into them the fruits of the law, he shall protect you in the time in which the Mighty One shall shake the entire creation (32:1).

Also, as for the glory of those who proved to be righteous on account of my law, those who possessed intelligence in their life, and those who planted the root of wisdom in their heart – their splendor will then be glorified by transformations, and the shape of their face will be changed into the light of their beauty so that they may acquire and receive the undying world which is promised to them. Therefore, especially they who will then come will be sad, because they despised my Law and stopped their ears lest they hear wisdom and receive intelligence (51:3-4).

For with your counsel, you reign over all creation which your right hand has created, and you have established the whole fountain of light with yourself, and you have prepared under your throne the treasures of wisdom. And those who do not love your Law are justly perishing. And the torment of judgement will fall upon those who have not subjected themselves to your power (54:13-14).

But you ought to know that our Creator will surely avenge us on all our brothers according to everything which they have done against us and among us; in particular that the end which the Most High is preparing is near, and that his grace is coming, and that the fulfilment of his judgement is not far. For now we see the multitude of the happiness of the nations although they have acted wickedly; but they are like a vapour (84:2-3). (All translated by Kljin, 1983).

The language is not all that different from that found in Matthew, both in the woes against the Pharisees, as well as in other warnings and challenges found throughout the Gospel. A good case can be made that Matthew's polemic is similar to that of his contemporaries.

Similarly, in 4 Ezra, the law is the way of affirming the righteous and dismissing others. The righteous are the people who keep God's commands and laws. The law is described as God's gift to Israel, which they have rejected, as have the wicked. A few examples will illustrate:

> Then I answered and said, "O sovereign Lord, behold, you have ordained in your Law that the righteous shall inherit these things, but that the ungodly shall perish (4 Ezra 7:17).

> Now this is the order of those who have kept the ways of the Most High, when they shall be separated from their mortal body. During the time that they lived in it, they laboriously served the Most High, and withstood danger every hour, that they might keep the Law of the Lawgiver perfectly (4 Ezra 7:88-89).

> For as many as did not acknowledge me in their lifetime, although they received my benefits, and as many as scorned my Law while they still had freedom, and did not understand but despised it while an opportunity of repentance was still open to them, these must in torment acknowledge it after death (4 Ezra 9:10-12).

> For behold, I sow my Law in you, and you shall be glorified through it forever. But though our fathers received the Law, they did not keep it, and did not observe the statutes; yet the fruit of the Law did not perish – for it could not, for it was yours. Yet those who received it perished, because they did not keep what had been sown in them. And behold, it is a rule that, when the ground has received seed, or the sea a ship, or any dish food or drink, and when it happens that what was sown or what was launched or what was put in is destroyed, they are destroyed, but the things that held them remain; yet with us it has not been so (4 Ezra 9:31-35, all translations from Metzger 1983).

These texts are included by way of illustration; the polemic of Matthew's Gospel in general, and Matthew chapter twenty-three in particular are by no means unusual or outliers in ferocity of attack or nature of the challenge. But that does not mean it is acceptable to continue to make polemical references, and the problem of how to preach from polemical New Testament texts remains. Moreover, the questions of context and dating must be considered. Scholars attempt to reconstruct both time, occasion and place of composition from a close reading of the texts; this is always speculative. Hence any use of contemporaneous polemic to understand Matthew's Gospel must be treated with caution.

John Kampen on Matthew within sectarian Judaism

Central to Kampen's (2019) argument is that Matthew's Gospel should be understood as a sectarian document. He uses the term "sectarian" in a technical, sociological, sense, of a small isolated fringe movement defining itself in opposition against a larger group. Thus, the polemic of Matthew, in Kampen's reconstruction, should be understood as a boundary marker, a means of defining who is within and who is a rejected outsider. Kampen relies particularly on the Dead Sea Scrolls to strengthen his case for the existence of first-century sectarian Judaism. That is not to say he argues for any kind of equivalence or close relationship between the Qumran community and the Matthean community. Rather, the Dead Sea Scrolls are a demonstration that there were sectarian groups present in first-century Judaism, even after the destruction of the temple. This makes it all the more plausible to argue that the Matthean community are also a sectarian Jewish group.

There are numerous polemical addresses of opponents throughout the Dead Sea Scrolls. Two examples will illustrate. The first is a short extract from a hymn in which the Teacher of Righteousness, the leader of the community, presents his opponents as persecutors and teachers of falsehood:

> But they are mediators of fraud and seers of deceit, they have plotted a devilish thing against me {...} to change your Law, which you engraved in my heart, for flattering teachings for your people; they have denied the drink of knowledge to the thirsty, but for their thirst they have given them vinegar to drink, to consider their mistake, so they may act like fools in their feasts so they will be caught in their nets. But you, O God, abhor every plan of Belial and your counsel remains, and the plan of your heart persists endlessly. But they,

hypocrites, plot intrigues of Belial, they search you with a double heart, and are not firmly based in your truth. A root which produces poison and bitterness is in their thoughts, with stubbornness of heart they inquire, they search for you among the idols, place in front of themselves the stumbling-block of their iniquities, they go to search for you in the mouth of prophets of fraud attracted by delusion (1 QHª XII: 9-16, in Martínez and Tigchelaar 1997,169).

Second, Johnson (1989, 440) gives two examples from the community rule, 1QS, which contain sections of polemical address against outsiders:

And the Levites shall curse all the men of the lot of Belial. They shall begin to speak and shall say: "Accursed are you for all your wicked, blameworthy deeds. May God hand you over to terror by the hand of all those who carrying out acts of vengeance. May he bring upon you destruction by the hand of all those who accomplish retributions. Accursed are you, without mercy, according to the darkness of your deeds, and sentenced to the gloom of everlasting fire. May God not be merciful when you entreat him. May he not forgive by purifying your iniquities. May he lift the countenance of his anger to avenge himself on you, and may there be no peace for you by the mouth of those who intercede" (1QS II:4-9, in Martínez and Tigchelaar 1997, 73).

However, to the spirit of deceit belong greed, sluggishness in the service of justice, wickedness, falsehood, pride, haughtiness of heart, dishonesty, trickery, cruelty, too much insincerity, impatience, much foolishness, impudent enthusiasm for appalling acts performed in a lustful passion, filthy paths in the service of impurity, blasphemous tongue, blindness of eyes, hardness of hearing, stiffness of neck, hardness of heart in order to walk in all the paths of darkness and evil cunning. And the visitation of all those who walk in it will be for an abundance of afflictions at the hands of all the angels of destruction, for eternal damnation by the scorching wrath of the God of revenges, for permanent terror and shame without end with the humiliation of destruction by the fire of the dark regions. And all the ages of their generations (they shall spend) in bitter weeping and harsh evils in the abysses of darkness until their destruction, without there being a remnant or a survivor for them (1QS IV:9-14, in Martínez and Tigchelaar 1997, 77).

As with the examples from other texts cited above, the level of vitriol is significant. There is no mistaking the fact that the person speaking dislikes his opponents and expects God to deal harshly with them. Indeed, the tone in the Dead Sea Scrolls appears harsher, more personal, more condemnatory than that found in much of Matthew's Gospel. Does that mean we can just say that Matthew 23 is of its time, and that we should not be overly concerned about the precise details of what Jesus says or the tone of the chapter as a whole? Clearly it does not, as the analysis to date has not dealt with the reception history of the texts. The Dead Sea Scrolls were discovered less than a hundred years ago, and their impact is limited outside of certain specialist academic circles. Matthew's Gospel, by contrast, has had a massive impact on the relationship between Christians and Jewish people for millennia. It is not simply what a text says, but how it is interpreted and used that matters.

Can we just say "its polemic"?

Levine and Brettler argue that polemics can be harmful, and words can be damaging and have devastating long-term consequences. But polemics may also have rhetorical merit, especially in clarifying the precise nature of the issues under debate (2020, 59). There is thus a value in recognising that Matthew's Gospel contains polemical texts, and that the purpose of the polemic is to establish boundaries and explain what it means to follow Jesus. Moreover, as Johnson argues, recognising that the polemic is primarily internally, not externally, focused, is a useful caveat.

But as Levine argues, there are problems with simply regarding the New Testament's polemical texts as "standard polemic" of the time. First, whilst the other texts cited remained internally focused, Matthew's Gospel became externally focused, and was shared widely with the gentiles. As a result, texts from Matthew, especially 27:25, were used as the primary justification for the massacre of Jewish people. Thus, although there may be echoes of the Hebrew Prophets' denunciation of Israel in the words of Jesus, the two are not equivalent, as the former remained internally focused whilst the latter became externally focused. The same can be said of the Apocryphal and Dead Sea Scroll texts cited above. They remained part of an internal, intra-Jewish argument, whilst Matthew's Gospel became a Christian text. Second, we must ensure there is an even comparison, looking at lots of texts from all sides of the debate. It might be the case that Matthew 23 is more moderate than Psalms of Solomon 4, for example, but in the balance of history, Christians were as (if not more) vitriolic about Jews as Jews were about Christians. Moreover, Psalms of Solomon is internally focused. But the same cannot be said of Matthew's polemic. Third, there is a risk that if this argument is followed to its logical conclusion, then Judaism and Jewish people are blamed for the polemic of the New Testament, and Christians escape taking responsibility for the failures of the past. Finally, Matthew, unlike other texts discussed here, "claims that the 'enemies' (however configured) *killed* the leader of their movement" (Levine 2002, 91). We therefore return to the question of power with which the chapter began. The issue is less what you say, and more how you are heard, and what actions flow from your words.

In conclusion

The main argument this chapter makes is that Christians must take responsibility for how they have abused sacred texts, and not just the texts of the New Testament. Matthew's Gospel frequently cites the Prophet Isaiah as part of the argument that Jesus fulfils the Jewish hope for a Messiah. In the medieval church, Isaiah came to be seen as more of a Christian evangelist than as a prophet to the people of Israel. Sawyer laments, "over and over again we find the Church choosing texts from Isaiah to prove how misguided the Jews are, and to authorise attitudes of arrogance and hostility towards them" (1996, 5). This is a frightening example of the misuse of a polemical text, especially given the imbalance of power between Christians and Jewish people both then and now.

Sawyer discusses how Isaiah was used to facilitate Christian antisemitism. His first example comes from an inscription over the door of a church in Rome, which has Isaiah 65:2-3a inscribed above the door. The text is also quoted by Paul in Romans (10:21), and reads

> All day long I have stretched out my hands to a rebellious people, who walk in a way that is not good, following their own devices; a people who provoke me to my face continually.

Sawyer points out that the reference is now to Jewish people, who are coming in and out of a ghetto, and "implies in strong biblical language that the Christians' God hates them." He adds that the inscription is accompanied by a fresco of Christ, "whose hands 'stretched out' on the cross clearly imply that it is Christ himself who is addressing the chilling words of Isaiah to the Jews" (1996, 100). This is but one of countless examples of Christian use of Isaiah to perpetuate hatred towards and condemnation of Jewish people. Sawyer argues that the history of Christian antisemitism is reflected in the use of Isaiah by the Church, in particular the condemnation of Jewish people for failing to recognise Jesus in Isaiah's prophecies of the Messiah.

This shift from Isaiah the Prophet of Israel to Isaiah the Prophet of the Christians is indicative of the language of the powerless being appropriated and used by the powerful. Sawyer identifies three stages in the debate between Jewish people and Christians. The first is internal to Judaism, commencing with Jesus' debates with the "scribes and Pharisees," focusing on questions of covenant, law, the status of gentiles, and the interpretation of scripture. In the second stage, as Christianity became more present within the Roman empire, it was inevitable that the missionaries, who presented themselves as the true Israel, would engage in polemics against the Jews. Third, over time Christianity was established as the mainstream religion, with its Bishops becoming figures of considerable power. At this point their writings were as much theological as polemical, and aimed at other Christians more than at Jews, who by now had little power or status (1996, 107-8).

To give one example: Isidore of Seville's *De fide Catholica adversus Judaeos*, written in the early seventh century, cites Isaiah in the context of expositing Matthew 27:25. Within Isaiah is the rebuke: "Prepare slaughter for his sons because of the guilt of their father" (14:20). This was used to chilling effect. Isidore changed the third person pronouns (his sons … their father) of the original Hebrew into second person pronouns (your sons … your father) in order "to make the application of Isaiah's invective to the contemporary situation more personal and biting" (Sawyer 1996, 113). In Isidore's use of Isaiah, the truth of the Gospel is present but the Jews, who read the text but do not understand it, condemn themselves by their own failure. Christians must reflect on the impact on Jewish people of their belief that the prophecies of Isaiah are fulfilled in Jesus (on which see Mayfield 2020, 2022).

Although the examples of the use of Isaiah come from a much later period than the first-century CE, they are included here to make the point plain: polemic is not simply words. Polemic can shape a worldview, which in turn can lead to hatred and even violence. We cannot simply say, it's just conventional (first-century) polemical language. A more robust response is required.

This chapter has surveyed the scholarly arguments about the polemic of the New Testament. I began by introducing Callaway's argument that there is plenty of polemic within the prophetic literature. The next discussion was of Johnson's exploration of the anti-Jewish polemic found in the New Testament. Johnson notes it is typical of its day, if not more moderate than the polemic found in other contemporaneous texts. This point was exemplified through citation of Apocryphal and Dead Sea Scroll texts cited by Overman and Kampen in their discussions of the polemic of Matthew's Gospel.

As Johnson argues, polemic can be understood, and explained, as primarily connotative not denotative, as indicating that opponents exist, rather than necessarily saying anything much about them. A related point is that polemic can be understood primarily as a boundary marker. That is, its function is to divide between in-group and out-group. The purpose is therefore not so much to condemn as to encourage people to remain committed. Third, polemic is often internally focused, used for critique of the in-group, not attack of the out-group. As we shall see, this is an interpretation adopted by many evangelical scholars when they exegete Matthew 23.

But whilst it is clear that polemic was an integral part of debate in the first-century, that does not solve the problem of abuse of polemical texts, as the examples of the misuse of Isaiah by Christians demonstrates. It is doubtless an important first step for Christian preachers to recognise polemic for what it is, but this is only a foundation for teaching and preaching, rather than the fitting conclusion. Subsequent chapters will discuss the preacher's task in greater detail; for the moment it is noted as unfinished business that Christians would do well to contemplate at length.

Chapter 4
Condemnation of the Pharisees: Matthew 23

The previous chapter examined the nature of first-century polemical debate. Whilst noting that the polemic of Matthew 23 can be considered simply as an example of a contemporaneous style of debate, it was also suggested that this is not a sufficient solution to the problems caused by misinterpretation of the chapter. It is all very well to say that Jesus was talking in the debate vernacular of his time, but how will that prevent his followers from continuing to use that vernacular? The purpose of this, and subsequent, chapters is to explore the rhetorically challenging passages in the Gospel of Matthew in more detail.

This chapter begins with a discussion the relationship between the Pharisees and the rabbis, noting also the work of Hilton and Marshall, and of Yarbro-Collins, before exploring the views of some scholars in the Matthew within Judaism school. Third, the expositions of six evangelical scholars are discussed before conclusions are reached about how to preach from Matthew 23 today. The chapter explores possible interpretations of Matthew 23 that mitigate or re-focus the polemic in such a way as to reduce or remove the potential for antisemitism. The primary strategy employed by evangelical scholars is to re-direct the polemic as a form of internal critique of the Christian church.

The relationship between the Pharisees and the rabbis

Before discussing interpretation of Matthew 23, it is first necessary to clarify the relationship between the Pharisees and subsequent rabbinic Judaism. Whilst some have, in the past, argued for continuity, the evidence is not actually that clear. What is clear is that the term "Pharisee" is loaded with all kinds of meanings, which it is important to recognise as we explore the interpretation of Matthew 23.

Neusner argues that Christians tend to condemn Pharisees as hypocrites or legalists (1984, 45). This latter belief has influenced the English language, so now "pharisaic" means "hypocritical, self-righteous" in general parlance. We must recognise this bias and not allow it to unduly influence historical enquiry into the actual beliefs and practices of first-century CE Pharisees. A similar point is made by Morrison, who contrasts unthinking condemnation of Pharisees with white actors wearing Blackface. Even if there is no intention to insult, the practice remains offensive (2021, 4).

Stemberger is cautious as to how historically accurate it is to argue for clear continuity from the Pharisees to modern rabbinic Judaism. He notes both first- and second-century textual evidence, which indicates opposition to the rabbinic perspective, as well as the inability of the rabbis to prevent the Bar Kokhba revolt in 132-35 CE. Stemberger traces the development of rabbinic theology and influence, making it clear that we cannot draw a direct and clear connection between the first-century Pharisees and subsequent rabbinic Judaism (2000, 78-92). Stemberger explains that early rabbinic texts rarely mention Pharisees by name; indeed, even the famous Shammai and Hillel have little historical attestation, and certainly not enough evidence to posit full continuity from Pharisees to rabbis. That is not to say there are no points of connection. Stemberger notes there were synagogues throughout the period in question, and that while Pharisees, and subsequently the rabbis, were active in synagogues, neither group can be conclusively proved to have controlled synagogues. Stemberger adds that it might be the case that the Pharisees' careful attention to interpretation of Torah influenced subsequent rabbinic exegesis, but this claim cannot be proved. A similar point could be made about transmission of religious ideas and oral tradition. Thus, while the Pharisees may have influenced the rabbis, they cannot be described as direct precursors (2021, 240-54).

Whilst we must be cautious about what relationships we posit with subsequent groups; we can still see Matthew's Gospel as one side of an argument about how to be an observant Jew in an era when the Temple is no more. And that argument was a highly polemical one, as the scholars discussed below explain. We must be aware of the impact of this language, as Hilton and Marshall make plain.

Hilton and Marshall on reading in the company of others

In their introduction to their study guide on the Gospels and Rabbinic Judaism, Hilton and Marshall note that even modern interfaith dialogue can all-too-easily become competitive, with all those participating aiming primarily to prove the superiority of their own faith position. Hilton and Marshall propose a better way is to engage with curiosity, and a desire to learn from the perspective of different faiths. This leads them to briefly discuss Matthew 23, focusing particularly on the use of the title "rabbi," which they argue was not, in fact, in use during Jesus' day, but only came to be used towards the end of the first century. Thus, they conclude, Matthew 23 is not so much a record of a sermon Jesus preached as an account of the struggle between groups in Matthew's own context, when the relationship between the early Christian and the Jewish community was beginning to deteriorate (1988, 1-4).

Hilton and Marshall explain that reading the Gospels is no easy task, but requires careful skill. For Christians, overfamiliarity may prevent the gaining of fresh insights. For Jews, "the uncomplimentary references to Jews and to rabbinic figures are a major difficulty" (1988, 13). Hilton and Marshall add that different texts are uncomfortable for different people; some they refer to are difficult for Jews, others are hard for Christians. But their main aim is that both Christians and Jews read all the texts together, as a means of entering into dialogue (1988, 35).

In Matthew 23:23, Jesus criticises the scribes and Pharisees for tithing herbs but ignoring the "weightier matters" of justice and mercy. Hilton and Marshall comment:

> The rabbinic texts are certainly concerned with close details: but the close study of such detail often reveals that the concern is to work out the principles of justice and mercy in practical terms: the rabbis

were committed to the belief that it is not a simple matter to say what is "just" and "unjust" in a particular situation (1988, 81).

The purpose of Hilton and Marshall's study is therefore to complicate and nuance the polemical rhetoric found within Matthew's Gospel, and indeed throughout the New Testament. In this particular case, their argument is that concern over minutiae does not necessarily indicate indifference to over-arching principles. Rather the converse is the case; it is through working through the nitty-gritty detail that the over-arching principles can be securely anchored in the practical realities of everyday living. Was Jesus aware of that point? Does Matthew agree that faith must find practical expression in the detail of day-to-day life? Even a cursory read of the whole of the First Gospel would give affirmative answers to these questions. So, Matthew 23 cannot be simply read as condemnation of legalism by a footloose and free teacher. The rhetoric must be more sophisticated than that; and it is to exploring that sophistication that I will now turn.

Adela Yarbro-Collins on polemic against the Pharisees in Matthew 23

Yarbro-Collins begins with an overview of scholarly views on the social setting of Matthew's Gospel. She discusses scholars who argue for a setting within Judaism, but rejects the proposal, arguing instead that the Matthean community was mixed, Jewish and Gentile, representing a wide variety of perspectives, ranging from those who strictly followed every stipulation of Torah to those who had a primarily Hellenistic understanding of virtue and ethics.

For Yarbro-Collins, the parable of the wicked tenants is the problem text for determining the first audience of Matthew. The particular issue is Jesus' statement that the kingdom of God will be taken from the scribes and Pharisees and given to a "people" who will bear its fruit (21:43). The crux is thus the interpretation of *ethnos*. For Yarbro-Collins, it does not mean a voluntary association or social group, but rather a new people, consisting of Jews and gentiles, cohering around faith in Jesus. Thus, the audience of Matthew is a mixed group:

the evangelist and likely audience of Matthew are like the community related to the Dead Sea Scrolls in articulating sharply polemical criticisms of rivals and outsiders. They are unlike them, however, in having a more flexible interpretation of the application of the Torah and in attempting to recruit members from among the gentiles (2021, 156).

Yarbo-Collins focuses on Matthew 23:13-36, arguing it presents both prophetic woes, which feature punishment, as well as sectarian woes. She notes prophetic woes appear in the Hebrew scriptures and in 1 Enoch 92-105, but argues the woes in Matthew have an additional sectarian focus. For Yarbro-Collins, the scribes and Pharisees of Matthew 23 "represent the leaders of Jewish communities with whom the evangelist and his fellow leaders competed for power and influence" (2021, 168). She believes this representative function has continued throughout history, so the Pharisees are taken as representing the Jews of the interpreter's day, an inaccurate understanding that has only recently been challenged. In this way negative stereotypes about Jews and Judaism were continually reinforced.

Yarbro-Collins warns against using this text to negatively characterise one's opponents and suggests Matthew 23 was written by Matthew, so he must bear at least some responsibility for the damage it has caused. She strikingly notes that in the Sermon on the Mount, Jesus warns that calling a brother a fool puts one in risk of the fire of Gehenna (5:22), yet in the woe sayings, Jesus calls the Pharisees "blind fools" (23:17). Yarbro-Collins suggests this latter text is a Matthean composition. But even if the woes do go back to Jesus, they can still be critiqued, for failing to attain the standard expected by the Sermon on the Mount.

This brief discussion has highlighted the importance of recognising the assumptions that we bring to the reading of any text. Reading with the eyes of faith, Christians will presume Jesus is always speaking truth. How does that impact our reading of Matthew 23? We must become aware of all our biases as we delve into this complex text.

Matthew within Judaism views

This section will explore the views of four scholars from the "Matthew within Judaism" school of interpretation. First, Saldarini's discussion of Matthew's own group and their opponents. Second, Kampen's view of the Matthean community as a sectarian group, and third, Overman's proposal that Matthew 23 is primarily a pedagogical text, teaching the Matthean community about the nature of true and false leadership. Finally, Gale's explanation that Jesus does not condemn all scribes is explained. All four attempt, in their own way, to limit the scope of the polemic, primarily by regarding it as part of an intra-Jewish argument. There are dangers in this approach; as Levine notes above, if taken too far, this strategy can mean Christians are left without culpability for the antisemitism of the church. But it is nevertheless a useful viewpoint that is worth exploring in greater detail.

Anthony Saldarini

Saldarini begins his discussion of Matthew's opponents by defining them as the leaders of Israel (Pharisees, scribes, chief priests, elders of the people, Sadducees and Herodians) who are "unequivocally rejected" (1994, 44). He reiterates his point that Matthew nowhere rejects Jews or Judaism, but only particular interpretations of Judaism, the leaders who promulgate those views, and occasionally those who follow those leaders. Saldarini offers a more rounded portrayal of the scribes and Pharisees in particular, noting that many of the questions they ask, about issues such as Sabbath observance, divorce, blasphemy, hand washing etc were legitimate areas of discussion within first-century Judaism. For Saldarini, Matthew's portrayal of those who oppose Jesus, and his vitriolic responses to them, are part of a wider apologetic effort to explain why it was that Jesus was crucified (1994, 44-45).

When he examines Matthew 23, Saldarini begins by arguing that the purpose of the chapter is to undermine the established Jewish leadership as a way of legitimating Matthew's own group and its leadership. He adds

The origin, structure, and tone of the attack on the Pharisees and scribes strongly indicate that Matthew is engaged in serious controversies with the Jewish community of his day and that he is attacking its leaders through Jesus' polemic (1994, 46).

Saldarini notes that even in the polemic of Matthew 23, there is no sense that Israel, its law or its community are illegitimate in and of themselves. Rather, the attack is against the leaders, their interpretation of the law and their actions, in order to establish a contrast and portray his own group in a more favourable light.

In order to further explore the purpose of Matthew 23, Saldarini discusses social scientific views of the process of legitimation and de-legitimation. He explains that people are first convinced of the way things are and then second, they affirm values that conform with their view of reality. Thus, if two groups are in conflict, especially if one is far bigger than the other, there is a tendency to rearrange one's group legitimations in order to reaffirm one's own symbolic universe and at the same time attack that held by the other group. This means that Matthew is not trying to destroy the whole symbolic universe of Judaism, but rather "proposing from within an alternative understanding of it and its actualization in life" (1994, 47).

The opening verses of Matthew 23 have troubled interpreters for generations. As Saldarini notes, while Jesus starts by acknowledging the authority of the scribes and the Pharisees, he then proceeds to undermine them by attacking their titles, laws and intentions, as well as proposing an alternative model of community leadership. For Saldarini, this is indicative of the conflict Matthew faces. He notes that one group that emerged as claiming authority in the post-70 era consisted of the successors to the scribes and Pharisees. This group, he proposes, were active in Matthew's area and rejected Jesus and his interpretation of the Law. Matthew is therefore mounting a counter-attack, charging them with hypocrisy and setting out his own model of how the community should be led.

Saldarini sees the polemic of Matthew 23 as one of a number of places in the Gospel where Matthew "exhibits the characteristics of a sectarian leader protecting his group from the dominant social institution and from rival sects" (1994, 49). The seven woes (23:13, 15, 16, 23, 25, 27, 29) use a technique similar to that of the Sermon on the Mount, contrasting inner attitude with outward behaviour. The woes focus on rival interpretations of community identity, attack prevailing interpretations of the law and challenge the personal ethics and intentions of the leaders, through charges of lawlessness and murder. Saldarini concludes that the vitriolic language and detailed accusations are suggestive of a Matthean attack on the leaders of his city. Matthew does this primarily to legitimate his own teaching and status, as well as delegitimating his opponents (1994, 46-52).

Matthew also attacks the Jerusalem leadership; chapters 21-22 contain symbolic actions that provoke, and then five controversy stories and three parables, all of which are part of this confrontation. Saldarini reads this wider attack as also being part of Matthew's attack on the leadership of the Jewish community of his day, who have themselves attacked Matthew's community, opposing his group and their interpretation of Judaism (1994, 52-64). Thus, for Saldarini, Matthew 23 is primarily internally focused, providing a boundary and encouragement to Matthew's small community of followers of Jesus. This understanding reduces the antisemitic potential of the text by limiting its applicability to the original context. As we shall see in the discussion of Kampen's views, the sectarian understanding is favoured by others in the Matthew within Judaism school.

John Kampen

Kampen explores the nature and significance of the Pharisees, Sadducees and scribes in depth (2019, 22-30). He begins with the Pharisees, noting there is not that much evidence as to their origin as a group. Kampen proposes they be understood primarily as an activist group that resisted the power of the aristocracy and agitated for their interpretation of the law to become mainstream. He concludes they were influential, and that they did have representation in both Galilee and Jerusalem, even amongst the chief priests. Kampen also notes that while Mark refers to the scribes, in Matthew, these references are primarily to the Pharisees, and that in the latter text, both groups indicate an educated elite that are in opposition to Jesus.

Turning to the rabbis, Kampen questions the scholarly consensus that there is a chain of transmission and heritage from the Pharisees to rabbinic Judaism. His argument is based primarily on the lack of evidence in the Talmud and the Mishnah for this link; most of the significant figures in rabbinic Judaism are never identified as Pharisees, and are not mentioned, for example, by Josephus. Kampen argues that

> all the evidence points to the rabbis as a scholastic group in the second century who studied Torah and worked at developing a model for the ideal Jewish life, however without any real power within the Jewish population as a whole (2019, 32).

Thus, in Kampen's view, far from being the direct descendants of the Pharisees, the rabbis were isolated individuals, who gradually over time gathered and grew in status, but not till well into the second century, if not later (2019, 30-34). This is an important point; the myth of a direct line of continuity from Pharisees to rabbis owes more to later speculation than to first-century reality.

When Kampen discusses Jesus and his opponents, he notes that the conflict begins when Jesus rides into Jerusalem on a donkey (21:1-11), and continues once Jesus returns to Jerusalem and the temple in the subsequent days. Kampen argues that to understand Matthew 23 we must first discuss chapters 24 and 25. He proposes that these chapters indicate that Matthew found parallels between the events of 66-70 CE and those under Antiochus Epiphanes in 167-64 BCE. There is thus, Kampen suggests, an apocalyptic focus to chapter 23, and the destruction of the temple cannot be far from the author's thoughts. Chapter 23 itself is clear evidence of the sectarian nature of the First Gospel, as Matthew

> marginalizes his immediate opponents by bringing them into the circle of the Jewish authorities and leaders who are held responsible for the destruction of the temple by some groups in the Jewish community (2019, 160).

The point is to draw a contrast between Matthew and his fellow followers of Jesus, who can rightly discern the will of God, and all others (scribes, Pharisees, Sadducees, chief priests, elders of the people), who cannot. The Pharisees in particular are singled out for condemnation, making unreasonable demands of the people (in contrast with Jesus' light demands and easy yoke, 11:30); loving praise and public recognition. Kampen also notes the parallels between the accusations of hypocrisy in relation to prayer and fasting in the Sermon on the Mount (6:2, 5, 16), and those found in chapter twenty-three, where an even more vigorous charge is made. Kampen also suggests parallels between the beatitudes (5:3-12) and the seven woes (23:13-36), concluding that the Sermon on the Mount sets out the agenda for Jewish followers of Jesus as the Messiah, while in chapter twenty-three, the opponents are described as the antithesis of Jesus' followers (2019, 158-167).

Kampen's main point is that the polemical rhetoric focuses on establishing clear boundaries for the Matthean sect as they demonstrate the righteousness of their cause and the failure of their opponents to correctly discern the will of God. Thus, the polemic of Matthew 23 is internally focused, and so cannot be directed externally at subsequent Jewish generations.

J. Andrew Overman

Overman proposes that Matthew 23 has a primarily pedagogical function, teaching the Matthean community the nature of true and false leadership. Overman understands "the scribes and Pharisees" as performing a representative function, indicating the leadership of Israel, with a particular focus on those whom the Matthean community oppose. This is a real and pressing struggle against a group whose leaders are murderers (23:29-39); hypocrites (23:13, 14, 15, 23, 25, 27, 29); fools and blind guides (23:16-17, 24); and inwardly corrupt and lawless (23:28). Overman argues that the polemical language of the chapter is common to other sectarian groups of the time, citing these other examples:

They devised for themselves vain thoughts,
and proposed to themselves wicked frauds;
they even declared that the Most High does not exist,
and they ignored his ways!
They scorned his Law, and denied his covenants;
they have been unfaithful to his statutes
and have not performed his works (4 Ezra 7:22-24, translated by
Metzger 1983, 537).

And you shall act lawlessly in Israel, with the result that Jerusalem
cannot bear the presence of your wickedness, but the curtain of the
Temple will be torn, so that it will no longer conceal your shameful
behavior .... You plunder the Lord's offerings; from his share you
steal choice parts, contemptuously eating them with whores. You
teach the Lord's commands out of greed for gain; married women
you profane; you have intercourse with whores and adulteresses.
You take gentile women for your wives and your sexual relations
will become like Sodom and Gomorrah. You will be inflated with
pride over your priesthood, exalting yourselves not merely by
human standards but contrary to the commands of God. With
contempt and laughter, you will deride the sacred things ... You
shall set aside the Law and nullify the words of the prophets by your
wicked perversity. You persecute just men: and you hate the pious;
the word of the faithful you regard with revulsion. A man who by
the power of the Most High renews the Law you name 'Deceiver,'
and finally you shall plot to kill him, not discerning his eminence; by
your wickedness you take innocent blood on your heads (*Testament
of Levi* 10:3; 14:5-8; 16:2-4 translated by Kee 1983).

As noted above in chapter three, the polemical language of these texts is
similar to that found in Matthew 23. But that does not equate to equivalence
in function or impact. These texts have not been held as sacred by billions
of people in the way that Matthew's Gospel has. Recognizing the
stereotypical nature of the language is a helpful, but insufficient, response
to the polemic of Matthew 23.

Overman is clear that Matthew regarded the threat to himself and his community as real; hence the sustained vitriol of the attack on the leadership of what was most likely the dominant, powerful group of the day. Matthew senses his community is losing traction with the wider Jewish community, and so is, Overman argues, letting off steam through Jesus' condemnation of the scribes and Pharisees. Matthew is not prepared to compromise; he does not want the followers of Jesus to be subsumed within the Judaism that is emerging in the aftermath of the destruction of the temple. Matthew provides a defence of his community's understanding and interpretation of the law, focused primarily on the person and actions of Jesus. His argument is that his fellow disciples of Jesus are the true Israel; they will be vindicated at the final judgement, while the leadership of "formative Judaism" will be condemned. Matthew's purpose is to force people to make a choice, either in favour of his views or against them. The purpose of the polemic of chapter twenty-three is that of the entire gospel, to make people respond to the claims of Jesus of Nazareth one way or the other (1990, 141-49). This "nothing to lose, say what you think" approach made perfect sense when the first followers of Jesus were a tiny embattled minority. But it had damaging longer term consequences as Christianity became more dominant over time.

In a subsequent book, Overman observes that modern Christianity has tended to avoid, rather than deal with, the problem these verses pose. He suggests that Christians who live "in such close historical and emotional proximity to the Holocaust shudder when reading this chapter," with the result that ecumenically minded Christians tend not to talk about such problematic passages (1996, 319). I would include interfaith conscious Christians within Overman's observation and respond that it is precisely because it is so troubling that it should become a feature of interfaith discussion. Indeed, the real issue is not so much the Holocaust as the centuries of European Christian antisemitism which created the conditions that enabled the Holocaust (Gerdmar 2009). Ignoring a problem never solves it; letting an issue fester almost inevitably makes it worse. It is far better to face up to the challenge head on.

Overman argues that the reality is that this chapter is simply an example of the rhetoric of its day. Overman notes that claims made by religions and religious communities are by their very nature exclusive and emotional, and Matthew 23 is no different. In this chapter Matthew makes it even more clear than he has already that "one cannot support the local leaders and still be a faithful Matthean Jew." His aim here is to further discredit and delegitimise the local religious leadership (1996, 319).

Overman mirror reads the situation of the Matthean community from this passage. Thus, Jesus' description of the scribes and Pharisees as sitting in Moses' seat is taken as indicating that the local religious leaders whom Matthew opposes are the ones with the political and judicial authority. The Matthean community must do what they say because of this reality, but at the same time, they are not to copy their actions, because the actions of the local leaders do not match up to their teaching (1996, 319-26). This is an entirely plausible reconstruction, but cannot be proved. It is certainly true that Jesus himself aroused opposition, so it is also quite possible that Matthew is simply reporting an earlier reality, rather than reflecting on his own context.

Overman proposes that Matthew is not bothered by the leaders' legislation or interpretation of the law. What he is concerned about is their hypocrisy. Thus, the polemic is equally focused on any Matthean Jew who does not wholeheartedly and fully obey the law. But the main point of the opening verses of chapter 23 is that those who oppose Matthew and his community have the positional authority. Overman argues that this "social and political reality" is useful for understanding the rest of the chapter. The Matthean community believes they are the ones who should be in charge, they should be the ones interpreting the law and they are the ones through whom the King (God) will exercise his rule (based in part on the parables of chapters 21 and 22). But, as Overman explains, they cannot do so. Instead, they must take instruction from those they believe are leading God's people astray. "In the struggle to decide who would lead and guide the people in the post-70 C.E. vacuum, Matthean Jews lost out in their setting. The bitter reaction to that reality is palpable in this chapter" (1996, 320).

The seven woes, which bring charges of blindness, hypocrisy and murder against the local leaders are given to discredit both their teaching and their character. They are accused of adhering to "human hierarchies and positions of honor" (1996, 321), loving the attention and deference of the public and titles and honours. Overman argues that the Matthean community was egalitarian but the local leaders encouraged a hierarchy which Matthew bitterly opposes, believing only God should have titles and honours.

Overman is particularly interested in the rejection of the title "rabbi." In the first-century it was primarily an honorific epithet, not a technical description of the role of a teacher. In Matthew it only occurs twice (26:25, 49), both times on the lips of Judas when he comes to betray Jesus. Overman suggests that "rabbi" was already associated with the enemies of the Matthean community, and this is why it is not used.

Overman concludes that Matthew associates the local leaders with the corrupt leaders of Israel's past. He discusses the reference to all the murders from Abel to Zechariah the son of Barachiah (Matthew 23:35), and concludes that the Zechariah referred to is probably a man murdered in the temple in 67 CE, as reported by Josephus in *Jewish Wars* 4.334-44. Overman explains that this indicates Matthew holds the local leaders responsible not only for the death of Jesus but also for "all the unjust murders in Israel," as well as the "chaos and destruction associated with the first Jewish revolt against Rome" (1996, 323).

Of course, Matthew was not the only person to link the leadership with the destruction of the temple. First-century Judaism, especially after the destruction of the temple, was fraught with polemical debate. "Matthew's was not a solitary voice claiming the local leaders are corrupt and that his group should soon be granted the opportunity to lead Israel in faith and truth. Indeed, first-century Palestine seems to be full of rivals for this claim" (1996, 325). The language in Matthew 23 is very stereotypical of this debate. Overman adds that this must have made it difficult for rival groups to compromise as they found themselves locked in an all-or-nothing confrontation.

Overman concludes his discussion of Matthew 23 with the observation that such "highly charged and derogatory language" is invariably deployed by the minority side in any debate. The point is that the Matthean community are marginalised and powerless, and are lashing out at those corrupt and compromised leaders whom they believe are guiding the people of God down the wrong path. With only their words to attack their opponents, Matthew's community gave it their all (1996, 326). The problem, of course, is that Christians are now in the majority, overwhelmingly so. Yet they still occasionally resort to using polemic language originally deployed by the tiny minority of Jesus followers. The issue is thus less about the nature of the language and more about the power and status of those who use it.

Aaron Gale

Gale discusses in some detail Jesus' condemnation of the scribes and Pharisees in Matthew 23. His first point is that the condemnation is very focused; and that Matthew has "coined a unique formula to indicate when he is discussing the leaders of the opposing formative Jewish community" (2005, 103). For Gale, in this chapter Matthew is not issuing a general condemnation of the profession of scribe, but rather making a defensive move to promote the scribes of the Matthean community and refute the alternative claims of rival scribes. Gale also points out that the sins Jesus condemns in Matthew 23 are also condemned by other contemporaneous rabbis. That is to say, "Matthew was just pointing out some of the inconsistencies in Jewish practice that offended his community" (2005, 103).

Gale cites an example from the Talmud of rabbis contradicting each other (*y. Berachoth* I 3a), which he presumes indicates Matthew is not condemning scribes as scribes, but rather castigating those he disagrees with. In Gale's reconstruction, the Torah is important to Jesus, to Matthew and his community. Thus, Jesus admonishes his disciples to respect all teachers of the law, but not to follow incorrect interpretations of the law. The problem is not that the opponents of Matthew's community do not know the law, it is that they interpret it wrongly (2005, 104-5). This limits the scope and impact of the polemic, but do modern exegetes recognise this?

Conclusions

The Matthew within Judaism school are at pains to soften the impact of the polemical rhetoric in chapter twenty-three. They do not deny that the language is harsh, but they limit its application to Matthew's immediate context, primarily by explaining the polemic as a minority defence mechanism, the last resort of a small group under considerable pressure. This is a commendable attempt at minimising the potential for this passage to be used to justify antisemitic words or actions. It does run the risk of reducing the issue to an entirely "Jewish" problem, allowing Christians to escape any culpability. Thus, whilst the explanation can be welcomed, it does not deal with the issue of Christian antisemitism entirely. With this problem in mind, it is instructive to note that at least some evangelical interpreters suggest the woes of Matthew 23 be directed primarily at a Christian audience.

Six evangelical views

Following the pattern set previously, this section will briefly discuss the expositions of R. T. France, Donald Hagner, Craig Keener, John Nolland, Tom Wright, and Martin Goldsmith, exploring four scholarly and two popular evangelical perspectives on Matthew 23.

R T France

Within his overview of Matthew's theology, France describes Matthew 23 as the most polemical passage in the Gospel and suggests, on the basis of the shift to address the "scribes and Pharisees" particularly, that Matthew wants to draw a distinction between the people as a whole and their leaders, for it is the latter who are condemned for their hypocrisy. He elaborates that the condemnation "is not so much a matter of the deliberate adoption of a false public image as of a casuistical concern for the minutiae of external behaviour which obscures rather than clarifies the essentials of how a man should aim to please God" (1989, 222).

France wonders whether the specificity of the target of condemnation therefore means that it is the leadership of the people of God, not the people themselves who are being replaced. He notes the "ludicrously incongruous touch" in the parable of the wedding banquet, where the king orders his soldiers to destroy the city of those guests who spurned his invitation (22:7). This, for France, is a clear indication that Matthew has linked the destruction of Jerusalem with the failure of the religious leadership (1989, 224). But this does not mean the people escape all responsibility. As the narrative develops, it is clear that those who throw their lot in with the leaders are equally culpable and will share the same fate. Thus, there is a process of continuity and discontinuity. Using the analogy of resurrection, he points towards a new body, that is still identifiable as related to the old, but at the same time qualitatively different. But this does not give Matthew's audience any reason to be smug or confident in their own status. Indeed, one of the aims of the Gospel is to warn its readers that they too could lose their place of privileged relationship with God if they fail to properly obey his Son and his teaching. This raises the question of replacement without rejection; is it possible for Christians to understand God to be doing a new thing in Jesus without rejecting what he has done, and continues to do, with and for the Jewish people?

In his subsequent commentary on the First Gospel, France suggests it is not "exegetically profitable" to attempt to distinguish between Jesus' attitude to the Pharisees and Matthew's attitude to the Judaism of his day, recognising that Jesus did get into sharp dispute with the Jerusalem leadership. France's reading is that Jesus' tone is indeed harsh, but his focus is not on individuals, but on the Pharisaic movement as a whole. He proposes that Jesus is condemning the Pharisees' collective failure to realise they were not actually doing God's will, for they were overly focused on detail at the expense of the big picture of divine priorities. He concludes the problems were by no means unique to the Pharisees, but rather "have their parallels in most religious traditions when the form comes to matter more than the substance" (2007, 854-55). This is a helpful caveat, allowing the interpreter to begin the rhetorical move away from potential antisemitism, towards an internally focused critique.

Discussing 23:1-12, France argues the discussion takes place in the temple courtyard, and the audience includes both Jesus' disciples and also the crowd, who are initially the primary focus of Jesus' warning about those who presume to teach. France describes the Pharisees and scribes as enjoying "popular respect and authority" as the recognised experts in the application of the Torah to the local context. He adds that Jesus respects this position, although the commendation might be ironic, given that Jesus subsequently challenges the Pharisees and scribes on the way in which they fulfil their role. In France's reading the two issues that concern Jesus are a failure to recognise the complications their teaching produces for ordinary people and their over-focus on appearance and reputation (2007, 858-59).

France proposes the focus shifts to the disciples in 23:8-12, warning against seeking status or public recognition. France argues Mathew includes this instruction because it remains a problem. He concludes:

> It is not difficult for a modern reader to think of similar honorifics in use today, and to discern behind the titles an excessive deference to academic or ecclesiastical qualifications (2007, 863).

For France, this passage is applicable in all times and places, from Jesus' day to today.

Turning to 23:13-36 France concurs with most commentators on seeing this section, together with Jesus' address to "the Jews" in John 8, as having the highest level of invective of any passage in the Gospels. France rejects the suggestion that Matthew 23 somehow "bookends" Jesus' public teaching (with the Beatitudes of Matthew 5 forming the first bookend). France regards the scribes and Pharisees as the main focus of Jesus' words. He proposes that the woes be understood both as condemnation of an over-focus on minutiae whilst neglecting the main purpose of the law, and also as condemnation of the scribes and Pharisees for failing to recognise that John the Baptist and Jesus were the true messengers of God. The result is condemnation and punishment, as divine judgement cannot be delayed any longer (2007, 867-82). Whilst France does correctly read the polemic of

Matthew 23 as internally focused, is he accurate in arguing it applies to all Pharisees? As we will see below, Hagner disagrees on this question at least.

Donald Hagner

Hagner divides Matthew 23 into four sections: an exhortation (23:2-12); seven woes on the Pharisees (23:13-33); a prophecy (23:34-36); and a lament (23:37-39). Of these four, the woes are clearly the centre-piece of the passage, and so any interpretation must both account for Jesus' harsh language and also mitigate against any potential antisemitic use of the text. Hagner is at pains to limit the scope of the woes, arguing they singled out only *some* Pharisees and were part of a debate according to the polemical conventions of the time. Moreover, the debate is a narrowly focused one of whether Jesus or the Pharisees are interpreting the law correctly. In Hagner's reading this is ultimately a Christological debate about the person of Jesus. He is clear that the passage is focused on a particular context and has no relevance to the Jews or Judaism of any other time, and that since it is polemical it cannot even be read as an objective description of Pharisaic Judaism (1995, 654-55). By way of background, Hagner cites from the Talmud, tractate *Sotah*, 22b, which includes this observation:

> The Gemara explains: The righteous of Shechem [shikhmi]; this is one who performs actions comparable to the action of the people of Shechem, who agreed to circumcise themselves for personal gain (see Genesis, chapter 34); so too, he behaves righteously only in order to be honored. The self-flagellating righteous; this is one who injures his feet, as he walks slowly, dragging his feet on the ground in an attempt to appear humble, and injures his feet in the process. The bloodletting righteous; Rav Nahman bar Yitzhak says that this is one who lets blood by banging his head against the walls because he walks with his eyes shut, ostensibly out of modesty. The pestle-like righteous; Rabba bar Sheila says that this is one who walks bent over like the pestle of a mortar (taken from sefaria.org).

For Hagner, this is another example of criticism of religious hypocrisy that is perhaps similar to what is found in Matthew 23. He does not address the question of timing, as the Talmud is a much later text; this question should be borne in mind, even if the main point, that religious hypocrisy has always been subject to criticism, still stands.

In his detailed discussion of the whole chapter, Hagner notes that Jesus respects the role of the scribes and Pharisees as interpreters of the Torah; what he is criticising are the points where he believes their teaching departs from the standards of the Torah. In particular, he condemns any desire to impress others or any love of prestige or position. Hagner recognises that these are issues which also impact Christians, and notes that Jesus warns his followers as well. But that does not hide the shocking nature of some of the text. Hagner describes 23:13-33 as "one of the most, if not *the* most, painful" text in the New Testament (1995, 672). He argues it probably does have a historical basis in the words of Jesus, who was, after all, opposed to the Pharisees and therefore is highly likely to have been critical of them. Hagner makes four additional observations: first, that this passage does not describe all Pharisees. Second, the material is gathered in one place by Matthew (the parallels in Luke are much more scattered, implying Jesus may have said them at different times). Hagner argues this increases their shock value. Third, although there is no word of grace in this passage, the Pharisees were not excluded from Jesus' invitation. Fourth, the woes were likely sharpened because of the intensity of the debate between the Matthean church and the synagogue. In Hagner's view, the only proper use of this passage today is to criticise neither historical nor contemporary Judaism, but solely as a means of criticising the Christian church (1995, 655-73). This is a helpful corrective move that Christian preachers and teachers would do well to adopt.

Hagner argues that the prophecy which follows the woes (23:34-36) primarily indicates the situation faced by Matthew and his church. Thus, the argument is that their Jewish contemporaries were just like their ancestors in that they killed those sent by God for their instruction. Finally in his lament over Jerusalem (23:37-39), Jesus indicates his desire that those he has castigated might be saved. If only they would repent, then that might be possible. Hagner sees this closing pericope as a warm burst of sunshine after the dark storm clouds of the rest of the passage (1995, 679-

81). There is always a need for hope in the midst of condemnation. Hagner's exposition is useful for limiting the scope of reference of the polemic, especially the rhetorical move to ensure it remains internally focused.

Craig Keener

Keener argues that the accounts of conflict with the Pharisees that are found in Matthew and John are likely to have their basis in Jesus' own life and ministry, proposing that at least some Pharisees must have joined with the Sadducees in persecuting Jesus and his first followers. There are multiple accounts of conflict over sabbath observance, so there is no reason to doubt that these took place. Keener recognises that Jesus' teaching was similar to that of the Pharisees, but explains that is no reason to presume there was no conflict. Indeed, he adds, conflict between those who are similar can often be the most severe (1999, 351-53). Keener explains the language of Matthew 23 as follows:

> The harshness of Matthew's language does not imply his alienation from his Jewish heritage – only from rivals for religious power within Syro-Palestinian Judaism. … The language of these woes reflects the regular conventions of ancient polemical rhetoric (1999, 536).

This explanation is similar to that utilised by other scholars and has been discussed at length, so I will not comment further on it at this stage.

Keener notes that the scribes and Pharisees are not the audience of the chapter, but merely a warning, "a negative paradigm." The audience are the disciples and the crowd. Keener disagrees with those preachers who create caricatures of Pharisees in order to avoid applying this text to Christians. As Keener explains, Matthew "appears to apply the warnings directly to his own community" (1999, 536-37). Keener thus adopts a similar strategy to Hagner.

In a brief excursus on the identity of the scribes and Pharisees, Keener explains that "scribes" cannot be a reference to the Jewish people as a whole. Rather it refers to a literate class who not only produced and dealt with documentation, but also educated children (and potentially adults), and some may have been priests or Pharisees. The term "Pharisee" is derived from one meaning "specifiers," that is, those who were precise in their adherence to and teaching of the Torah. In this he appears to follow an argument made by Schwartz in the Jewish Annotated New Testament, who argues Pharisees "probably derives from the Hebrew root *p-r-sh* (in the sense of 'specify')" (2017, 615). The alternative, and more popular, theory, is that it derives from "the Aramaic *perish,* pl. *parishaya,* Hebrew *parush,* pl. *perushim,* 'separate,' or, in this usage, 'separatists'" (Schiffman 2017, 619). Keener argues the Pharisees emphasised in particular obedience to the purity laws. They had considerable power, primarily because of their popularity rather than any formal position, although there were some individuals who were members of Jerusalem's municipal aristocracy (1999, 537-40).

Returning to his exposition of Matthew 23, Keener suggests the Matthean community may have still included some scribes and even Pharisees; thus, Matthew is sensitive to the Jewish orthodoxy of his audience, but not to their alienation from the Pharisaic leadership, with whom they are already in conflict. The points Jesus makes are that religious leaders should live out what they teach; they must not seek out badges of honour, honoured treatment or titles; and concentrate on exalting God. Keener entitles his discussion of 23:13-32 as "woes against human religion," a carefully chosen phrase to indicate this is an address aimed at the Matthean community, not at the Pharisees. Keener adds that Pharisees were considered to be "the most devoted practitioners of religion" and the scribes were regarded as "Bible experts" (1999, 547). The point of the woes is to explain that religious leaders can do more harm than good; that the unnecessary swearing of oaths or otherwise being inconsistent in attaining standards of holiness is dishonouring to God; and that religious leaders can mistakenly emphasise holiness in detailed matters whilst ignoring the big picture. The final point is that the bloodguilt for killing God's spokespeople will result in divine judgement (1999, 540-54). This is a helpful approach for teachers and preachers, provided it is always integrated with the internal focus noted above. That is to say, the purpose of the polemic is to encourage critical self-reflection, not as the basis for attacking others.

The final section of the chapter, 23:33-39, is discussed under the theme of impending judgement on the established religious leaders. Citing examples of how previous religious elites have killed God's messengers, from the first murder of Abel, to the murder of Zechariah as recorded in the final book of Chronicles, Jesus castigates those who will kill him, saying the bloodguilt for that murder will fall on them as it has on previous generations. Jesus then laments the pain of rejection and the destruction of Jerusalem that will inevitably follow (1999, 554-59). Keener discusses options for understanding the identity of Zechariah. Overman's view, that the Zechariah referred to by Matthew is identical to the one mentioned in Josephus' *Jewish Wars*, dates back to Chrysostom. Keener rejects this on the basis that this Zechariah was not a prophet. Keener is equally unconvinced Matthew is referring either to John the Baptist's father or to some "unknown Zechariah." Rather, in Keener's view, Matthew conflates Prophet Zechariah whose murder is recorded in 2 Chronicles 24:20-22 with the Prophet Zechariah who wrote the book Zechariah (1999, 556).

Keener's exegesis is useful, even if I do not agree with him entirely. It is hard to see how Cain can be described as a member of the religious elite, for example. Keener's etymology of "Pharisees" is also open to question. But his main point, that any polemic should be internally focused, is arguably the best interpretative approach.

John Nolland

In his introduction to the woes in Matthew 23, Nolland argues that part of the problem is, perhaps, that what was an address *to* a group of people has been read as a description *of* them. Thus, a context-specific address has been misread as a character analysis for all time. Moreover, we must read it within the conventions of first-century polemical debate, not according to the conventions of twenty-first century discourse (2005, 921). This is a reprise of Johnson's connotative not denotative argument; that is, the polemic tells us there are opponents. But it does not tell us much about them.

Nolland regards the crowds as the main audience, although the scribes and Pharisees remain present, as evidenced by the second person addresses towards them. They are understood as embodying the law; Jesus does not challenge their knowledge, merely their interpretation. Nolland explains the scribes and Pharisees are condemned for failing to care for those who struggle to fulfil the interpretation of the law that they, scribes and Pharisees, have promulgated. They are attention seeking, loving grand titles. Jesus warns his followers to not seek similar titles for themselves; thus, the warning against calling someone "father," is not directed at address to a male parent or respected elder, but rather against using the term as a title and a badge of authority (2005, 922-29).

Turning to 23:13-33, Nolland argues the scribes and Pharisees are now addressed directly. As with the other commentators discussed in this section, Nolland reads Jesus' condemnation as being of hypocrisy, of over attention to minor details without acknowledging the main principles of Torah, a desire to better oneself and a failure to recognise the purposes and work of God in John the Baptist and in Jesus himself. Thus, the scribes and Pharisees are condemned for not recognising the messengers of God, and so they, and Jerusalem, will suffer the divine punishment which follows as a logical consequence of that choice. God will withdraw from the temple; Jesus will be removed. Jesus hopes for a better future; once hearts have changed, he will be welcomed with joy (2005, 932-53).

Whilst Nolland helpfully points out that the woes are not a description of the Pharisees, his exegesis still raises questions, especially when he reads too much into the specifics of the text. This is a danger all Christian preachers and teachers must watch out for; if the polemic is not denotive, what level of detail can we draw from it?

Tom Wright

Wright begins his discussion of Matthew 23:1-12 by noting the parallels that have already been established between Moses and Jesus. He suggests that the scribes and Pharisees were guilty of talking a lot about Moses, interpreting and adding to the Torah, but did not necessarily live up to those stipulations themselves. The charge Jesus levels, therefore, is primarily one of hypocrisy; that whilst the focus was in the right place, the actions that should have followed, including focus on love and mercy, were sadly absent. Wright concludes that whilst this is a critique of abuse of religious authority, it is in fact wider ranging than that, as the Pharisees were also social and political leaders. He is clear that this critique can be applied today both to those in positions of leadership in the church, but also to wider society as well (2002b, 98-100).

The condemnations that follow (23:13-22) are explained as a criticism of the Pharisees for valuing the objects people have brought into the presence of God more highly than God's presence itself. This means they demonstrate their own failures. Wright is caustic in his criticism:

> They are like someone who has never learned to read trying to settle a dispute on the relative merits of Shakespeare and Goethe. They show by their every ruling that they simply don't know what they are talking about (2002b, 103).

Wright is well aware of the danger of this text being misused. He is clear that it cannot be taken as indicative of the Jewish people as a whole, either then or now. Whilst recognising (inaccurately) that the Pharisees were the precursors to rabbinic Judaism, Wright argues that Jesus' critique is very much of the moment, aimed specifically at those who "were leading Israel astray, causing Israel to look in the wrong direction, at the very moment when its hour, and indeed its Messiah, had come." The concern is thus not about the Pharisees per se, or about a particular way of responding to the Torah. Rather it is concern that those who were supposed to be guides for Israel were missing the crucial moment of God's work in sending the Messiah. Wright is equally clear that there is no need to read into this text a veiled criticism written by the Matthean community of their own contemporaries. Rather, Jesus knows he is being fiercely opposed, and is simply responding with his own counter-attack (2002b, 103-4).

The second set of woes (23:23-33) are discussed as indicating an outward conformity that masks an inner decay; the Pharisees and the scribes knew what they ought to do, they just weren't doing it. Like the earlier section, this condemnation only makes sense as part of the bigger picture. Jesus is attempting covenantal renewal through his own obedient life and death, something that the Pharisees cannot achieve, however much they intensify their obedience to the Torah. Wright argues that therefore this chapter must not be read as moral denunciation, and definitely not as moral denunciation of another. Rather it is to be read as pointing towards the restoration of relationship with God that only Jesus can achieve (2002b, 106-7).

The third section of the chapter (23:34-39) is understood as indicating judgement on Jerusalem and its leaders. Wright describes how a hen protects her chicks:

> There have been recorded instances of a mother hen, faced with a fire, collecting her young chickens under her wings to keep them safe. Sometimes she is successful: when the fire has done its worst and died down, you may find a dead hen with live chicks underneath its wings (2002b, 109).

If Jesus is the hen and his fellow Jews are the chicks, what is he saying? Wright argues that the fire is symbolic of the judgement that must fall if the people continue to reject God's prophets and are guilty of shedding innocent blood. He explains that this includes Israel who far from following her vocation to be light to the nations has in fact succumbed to the darkness of the world. Jesus longs to be the mother hen who shields her chicks whilst she herself dies, but they refused and so suffered the punishment when it fell (2002b, 108-10).

This third section is helpful; the image of the mother hen dying to save her chicks is a great exposition of the Christian belief that Jesus' death on the cross is somehow redemptive for all who trust in him. But Wright's earlier sections lack nuance. He appears to take the text as descriptive and does not mitigate against any potential antisemitic interpretations. This is all the more problematic in a popular exposition of the text. As subsequent chapters will show, a judiciously phrased sentence or two is a vital counter-balance to potential negative readings of these complex texts.

Martin Goldsmith

Goldsmith's discussion of the seven woes against the Pharisees begins with the observation that Jesus is talking to his disciples and the crowd, not to the Pharisees themselves. Jesus acknowledges the Pharisees have authority because of their teaching role, but criticises them for not following their own teaching. They are accused of legalism, seeking public honour and titles that are entirely unnecessary. Goldsmith then states that the same issues have plagued the Christian church down the centuries; singling out Anglican Canon Law as an example of unnecessary extra rules or the desire for titles and status, that have given rise to undue deference to bishops or other clergy, and pride amongst those in positions of authority in the church. Goldsmith suggests there are seven woes as a sign of completeness, with 23:14 being added due to the influence of Mark 12:40, as it is not found in some early manuscripts. Goldsmith also discusses 23:15, with its comments on Jewish proselytising. He suggests Matthew mentions it only in passing, because he did not believe it was necessary for gentiles to become Jewish in order to become followers of Jesus. The discussion concludes with Jesus' tears over Jerusalem; Goldsmith suggests he weeps because he knows what is to come and that judgement will be real (2001, 163-66). This is a good example of an accessible exposition that recognises the antisemitic potential of the text.

Discussion and conclusions

As noted above, a feature of the evangelical expositions of Matthew 23 is that the negative rhetoric is primarily directed internally, that is, against fellow Christians. At times this reads like point scoring against a denomination or perspective that the author personally disagrees with, as with Goldsmith's criticism of Anglicanism for example. But the main point appears to be that stated forcefully by Hagner, namely that if a Christian is to apply Jesus' woes to the contemporary context it is in self-reflective criticism, not in condemnation of those outside Christianity, least of all Jewish people. In the Gospels, not least in Matthew, Christ is clear that he has the role of judge, which he will fulfil at the end of time (a theme that is particularly clear in chapter 25). Judgement, praise and condemnation are all Jesus' remit, not mine.

This approach, of directing the negative rhetoric towards oneself and one's fellow Christian believers, will necessarily be rooted in a clear exegesis of the original context, and the proposals of the Matthew within Judaism school of interpretation are useful in this regard. They allow a teacher or preacher to explain that the text under discussion is part of an internal argument within Second Temple Judaism (or immediately post-temple Judaism, depending on what date one accepts for Matthew, and the extent one believes Matthew is really writing primarily about his own context). It is also useful to caveat this with recognition that the woes are typical of the polemical style of debate of the time. But it is the next rhetorical move that is crucial. Having established a Jewish setting for the first time Jesus spoke these words, one must at all costs avoid the implication that this means the Jewish people are somehow culpable for the rhetoric. This is why an immediate shift to self-reflection, coupled with a recognition of the role of Jesus as judge, is helpful. But as well as being challenged by Jesus' own rhetoric, it would also be necessary to reflect, even if only briefly, on the history of interpretation of this passage. For it is only by recognising how the text has been abused that we can begin to heal the hurts caused and avoid repeating the shameful mistakes and prejudices of Christians of previous generations. And if that is true of interpreting Matthew 23, it is even more vital for understanding Matthew 27:25, the verse under consideration in the next chapter.

Chapter 5
The Blood Cry: Matthew 27:25

In this chapter, I will be discussing what is arguably the most dangerous and devastating verse in the entire New Testament. The central focus is exploring explanations of what Matthew meant by writing that all the people cried "His blood be on us and on our children." After some a brief recap of the devastating history of interpretation of this verse from Levine, there follows a narrative-critical exposition from Heil; a discussion of "innocent blood" from Sider-Hamilton; Konradt's views on the crowds; the approach of the Matthew within Judaism school; and the expositions of the six evangelical commentators discussed previously.

As Levine explains:

> The verse that has caused more Jewish suffering than any other in the Christian Testament is the uniquely Matthean cry attributed to "the people as a whole": "His [Jesus'] blood be on us and on our children!" (27:25). This verse is often read as implying that all Jews, of Jesus' time and forever afterward, accept the responsibility and blame for Jesus' death. Christian Europe witnessed centuries of pogroms promulgated by church members, inflamed by sermons about the Jews' "blood guilt," who rushed to Jewish homes (often in ghettos established by Christian governments) to avenge their Lord. While the violence has mostly subsided, the charge remains. I have been accused of being a "Christ-killer"; so have my children (2002, 91).

Levine is clear in her mind that the whole scene has no basis in history; this is theology not history. She argues that there is no evidence of Pilate releasing prisoners – indeed the evidence points the other way, towards his callous disregard for Jewish sensitivities. Levine states that it is not possible for "the people as a whole" to shout for Jesus' death, because the category "the Jews" included the women from Galilee and Joseph of Arimathea, amongst others. Levine is clear that the geographical designations – Galilee and Arimathea – hint as to the focus of Matthew 27:25; it is aimed primarily at the fate of Jerusalem (2002, 92).

Levine regards Matthew as taking an anti-Jerusalem stance, and this verse is indicative of that view. For Matthew, along with other Jewish followers of Jesus, interpreted the destruction of Jerusalem as a just punishment for the rejection of Jesus. Levine adds:

> By speaking of the blood on Jerusalem's children, the Gospel reflects a specific past; it does not predict, let along enjoin, a global future. Today the verse is sometimes taken as a hopeful wish that Jews will accept the blood of Jesus. Unfortunately, this less violent interpretation may be just as pernicious. If all Jews proclaim the atoning death of Jesus the Messiah, the verse will have the same anti-Jewish effect: there would be only the *ekklesia*; there would be no more "Judaism" (2002, 92).

Thus, even the apparently benign interpretation, of wishing Jewish people would accept the salvific value of Jesus' atoning death, has the potential to be antisemitic.

The aim of this chapter is first to set out some of the possible interpretations of Matthew 27:25, and through doing so to explore whether it is possible to preach from this verse a genuine message of Christian good news. As is clear from the quotes above, Levine is sceptical (see also Levine 2006, 99-102). But perhaps it is possible. Levine and Brettler argue for the importance of critical historical analysis, coupled with ethical reflection, as a means of avoiding anti-Jewish or antisemitic interpretation. There are always choices made when we read and interpret texts, and we have a duty to do so responsibly (2020, 420-21).

This chapter is an attempt at such responsible exegesis and interpretation. It begins by surveying the arguments of Heil, Hamilton and Konradt, before returning to the views of scholars from the Matthew within Judaism school, as well as the six evangelical commentators whose views were discussed in the previous chapters. The main focus is on sensitivity to the power-relations that lie behind the text, as well as ways in which exegetes seek to minimise the impact of the polemical rhetoric.

John Paul Heil: A narrative-critical reading of Matthew 26 to 28

Heil's work is in the genre of reader-response criticism, and as such he is primarily interested in the "rhetorical effect" the text has on the implied reader rather than historical accuracy (1991, 1). Heil begins by briefly discussing the conflict with the Jewish authorities. He notes this starts in the infancy narratives, as Herod, with the help of the chief priests and scribes (2:4) seeks to murder the baby Jesus, new-born king of the Jews (2:1-18). As Jesus dies, the chief priests, scribes and elders all mock him as the king of Israel (27:41-42). The charge against Jesus, which ultimately leads to his execution, is that of blasphemy, which is first heard when Jesus heals the paralytic (9:3). Heil notes that disputes over the temple are central to the disagreement with the Jewish authorities, and that the opposition does not cease with Jesus' death (1991, 16-17).

Heil discusses 27:15-26 under the title "Jewish people accept guilt for the death of the innocent Jesus." He begins by noting that Pilate offers to release Jesus (27:15-18), explaining that the prospect of the apparently notorious Jesus Barabbas (literally "son of the father") being released adds to the dramatic tension. Pilate offers the crowd the chance to "accept as their true 'Christ' the innocent Jesus whom their leaders want to kill" (1991, 74). But the response of the crowd is to demand that Pilate crucifies Jesus (27:19-23). While Pilate's wife warns him to have nothing to do with the death of an innocent man, the Jewish authorities are persuading the crowd to call for Pilate to have him executed. In this they are successful, as the crowd demand the release of Barabbas. In the third main section (27:24-26), the people then invoke Jesus' blood upon themselves. Pilate withdraws from any personal responsibility. Heil argues for resonance with a ritual recorded in Deuteronomy 21:1-9. According to this stipulation, if a corpse was found between two cities, the elders of the city closest to the corpse must take a heifer that has never worked and break its neck in the place where the dead body was found. After the priest has pronounced a blessing,

> All the elders of that town nearest the body shall wash their hands over the heifer whose neck was broken in the wadi, and they shall declare: "Our hands did not shed this blood, nor were we witnesses to it Absolve, O LORD, your people Israel, whom you redeemed; do not let the guilt of innocent blood remain in the midst of your people Israel." Then they will be absolved of blood-guilt. So you shall purge the guilt of innocent blood from your midst, because you must do what is right in the sight of the LORD (Deuteronomy 21:6-9).

Pilate is also linked to Judas, who when he repents, recognises he has sinned in betraying "innocent blood."

Heil sees the cry of "all the people" in 27:25 as indicating corporate responsibility. He contrasts the willingness of the people with the refusal of the leaders to accept responsibility for the price paid to Judas (27:6-10), and argues the people are representative of "the entire covenant people of Israel (1:21; 2:6; 4:16, 23; 13:15; 15:8; 26:5)" (1991, 76). Heil sees the cry of 27:25 as fulfilling Jesus' prediction in 23:35 that all the righteous blood shed upon the earth will come upon them. He also notes there is an irony in the covenant people of Israel's cry as they inadvertently invoke Jesus' promise of the blood of the covenant poured out for many for the forgiveness of sins (26:28). This means the Jewish people inadvertently establish the salvific value of Jesus' blood, and place themselves and their successors in line to benefit from it. But despite this glimmer of hope, Heil is negative in his assessment of the impact of this choice on the Jewish people. He explains they not only accept the responsibility for shedding innocent blood, but also pay the price for doing so, by losing their "special prerogative as a people to the kingdom of God," which will now be given to those who will produce fruit (21:43) (1991, 73-77).

Heil's reading is a hard one; rejection of Jesus is understood as rejection of God. This raises all kinds of questions. Does this apply to all Jews for all time? To a limited number of Jewish people for a discrete amount of time? Are other readings of the text possible?

Catherine Sider-Hamilton on innocent blood

Sider-Hamilton contrasts two ways of reading Matthew 27:25. The first, more established, understanding is that this is an invocation of judgement upon Jerusalem. There are differences as to whether that sentence was specific to that particular generation, or more long lasting, but the overall tone is of destruction. Second, the "ironic" reading – that the angel tells Joseph that Jesus is the one who will save his people from their sins (1:21); Jesus himself tells his disciples blood is poured out for the forgiveness of sins (26:28). Thus, when the people say "His blood be upon us," they're actually invoking their own salvation. Sider-Hamilton recognises these two readings appear mutually exclusive, but wonders whether Matthew's focus on Jesus' "innocent blood" might provide the hermeneutical key to reconcile them (2008, 83-84).

The first point in Sider-Hamilton's argument is that "innocent blood" (Deuteronomy 21:8-9) is a trope within Matthew. It is founded in Pilate's declaration that he is innocent of Jesus' blood (27:24); earlier in the chapter Judas has also said he has sinned in betraying innocent blood (27:4). Further back in the Gospel, Jesus' final woe to the Pharisees places upon them "all the innocent blood shed upon the earth, from the blood of Abel the righteous to the blood of Zechariah" (23:35). Sider-Hamilton's case is that Jesus' death is a matter of innocent blood, part of a history of innocent blood that begins with Abel's murder by Cain (2008, 85-86).

Sider-Hamilton's second point concerns the legend of Zechariah's blood as developed within the rabbinic literature. The story is based on the death of Zechariah ben Yehoyada (2 Chronicles 24:20-22). Sider-Hamilton cites the account as follows:

> The setting is the fall of Jerusalem. Nebuzaradan, captain of the Babylonian guard, descends upon the city, leaving devastation in his wake. In the temple, he sees the blood of Zechariah seething and asks

what it is. At first the people tell him that it is the blood of sacrifices; he promptly slaughters animals but the blood still seethes. In a rage, Nebuzaradan hangs some of them – or, in the Babylonian version, threatens to tear their flesh with iron combs – and so they confess: "This is the blood of a priest and prophet and judge who prophesied to us all that you are doing to us and we arose against him and slew him." Nebuzaradan promptly slaughters the people upon the altar: in the Jerusalem Talmud, 80,000 young priests; in the Babylonian version, 940,000 men, women, and children – "and still the blood boiled. Thereupon Nebuzaradan became angry with Zechariah. He said to him: 'What do you want? Should we kill your whole people for your sake?' Thereupon the Lord was filled with compassion and said: 'if this man, who is but flesh and blood and is cruel, is filled with such compassion for My children … how much more should I be so.' Accordingly, He made a sign to the blood, and it subsided into its place" (*y. Taan. 69ab*). (Sider-Hamilton 2008, 86).

Sider-Hamilton notes that the legend persists throughout history, and can be traced to the early first century CE, to the Jewish text *The Lives of the Prophets*. The key elements of the legend are: blood poured out, death near the altar and retribution on the temple, none of which are in the original account in 2 Chronicles. Sider-Hamilton argues these same elements are present in Matthew's account of Zechariah's death, where he is recorded as dying "between the sanctuary and the altar" as his blood is poured out with particular responsibility for that death resting on the generation Matthew addresses. Finally, the account in Matthew might be linked to the destruction of Jerusalem via Jesus' lament over the city (23:37-38), which precedes the prediction of the destruction of the Temple.

In Sider-Hamilton's interpretation, both the legend of the death of Zechariah, and Matthew 23:35 are reflections on the fate of Jerusalem. This is a fairly common feature of both Jewish and Christian literature of the late first-century, as the destruction of the Temple was a devastating event within the religious life of the Jewish nation. Sider-Hamilton suggests that he is linked with Abel because in both cases, it was their innocent blood that cried out. She explains:

In this emphasis on blood, Matthew and the midrashim place the death of Zechariah, and that of Jesus, within a complex of ideas that has to do with pollution and expiation, the sanctity and danger of blood, and the defilement of the land (2008, 91).

This issue of innocent blood is present throughout the Hebrew Scriptures, as well as later Jewish writings. As Numbers 35:33 explains, blood pollutes the land, and unexpiated blood renders the land barren; "the blood of the innocent shed by anyone within Israel brings blood down on the whole people's head" (2008, 92). Further examples of this understanding include Hosea's warning that priests commit murder (Hosea 6:9); a point echoed in Isaiah (1:15; 59:7), Jeremiah (7:4-15; 19:4-5; 22:17), and Ezekiel ("woe to the bloody city!" 24:6, 9). Thus, Sider-Hamilton concludes, disaster on Jerusalem is not merely destructive judgement, but purging: "Innocent blood stains Israel and explains the destruction of Jerusalem: the land is defiled; it vomits it's people out and must be cleansed" (2008, 94). The legend of Zechariah brings the temple into particular focus within this wider understanding.

Sider-Hamilton argues that Matthew's account of Jesus' life and death is set against this backdrop. Thus, the people's cry in Matthew 27:25 is linked to the innocent blood of Zechariah (23:35). Jesus is twice called innocent (27:4, 19) and his blood shed on the cross parallels Zechariah's blood poured on the earth. Moreover, Judas' final act of throwing the silver he received for betraying Jesus onto the floor of the temple stains it just as Zechariah's blood did. "The theme of uncleanness continues: the priests, realizing that they cannot put blood money in the temple treasury, buy with it a burying ground for foreigners" (2008, 96). The place is even called "the field of blood" (27:8).

Pilate's act in washing his hands in innocence of Jesus' blood is, in Sider-Hamilton's understanding, a declaration that Pilate finds Jesus to be innocent of all charges, and thus "he names Jesus' condemnation a matter of innocent blood and bloodguilt, of the pollution that defiles land and people alike" (2008, 98). This brings the nation's survival into question, for a holy God cannot live amidst pollution, and the innocent blood must be expiated, or else the land will become barren, leaving the nation exposed before her enemies as the Lord departs the temple. The people, in their cry of responsibility, choose "blood guilt rather than absolution" (2008, 98). They thus take upon themselves the responsibility for shedding innocent blood which results in the conquest and destruction of the Temple in 70 CE.

In her conclusion, Sider-Hamilton notes that the Zechariah legend is purgative. There are still grounds for hope; a hope that is also present in Matthew. Hamilton finds that hope particularly in the fact that when Jesus dies, the curtain of the Temple is torn in two and the tombs are opened and the holy ones rise to life; thus, the angel's promise of salvation has been realised. Sider-Hamilton explains that

> the temple's desolation coincides with the tombs opening and the dry bones of Israel walking again (27:52). Destruction and re-creation come together in Matthew's vision and in the paradigm of innocent blood (2008, 99).

This means, Sider-Hamilton argues, Matthew's understanding is a thoroughly Jewish one. There is a new covenant made through the shedding of Jesus' blood, which is poured out "both for the destruction of the temple and the covenant people and for their restoration" (2008, 100). Matthew's argument is that with the destruction of the temple, the glory of God's presence now resides in Jesus, through whom the faith of Israel receives a new outworking and mission. It is a different understanding from that of the rabbis, who saw God's glory as residing in the Torah, but it is nevertheless still a Jewish framework of interpretation.

Sider-Hamilton works hard to blunt the impact of 27:25. But as Levine notes, presumed salvation is potentially offensive. Arguing that Jewish people are saved by Jesus' blood even if they do not realise this may comfort the Christian, but how does it make the Jewish person feel? The key question is, how do you treat those who reject Jesus? This question is especially pertinent in any context where Christians are in the majority vis-à-vis Jewish people.

Matthias Konradt: the crowds

Konradt begins by describing Matthew as a story of conflict, a conflict that mirrors the experience of the Matthean communities. Konradt reads that conflict as internal to Judaism, and argues that the crowd in Matthew is a distinct character in the narrative, clearly different to the authorities. That is not to say he understands the crowd to be a unified or uniform group throughout the narrative, but rather than Matthew uses the crowd in particular ways throughout his narrative.

Konradt's argument is in four parts. First, he examines the differentiation between the authorities and the crowds, arguing that Matthew distinguishes between the positive reactions of the crowds and the more hostile responses of the authorities (contrast 9:32-34; 12:22-24 for example). Moreover, Jesus is sent (and initially sends his disciples) to the lost sheep of the house of Israel, who stand in contrast to the shepherds, who failed to tend the flock (see Jeremiah 23:1-6; Ezekiel 34). Second, the crowds react positively to Jesus and display developing Christological insight. The crowds are warm to Jesus' teaching (7:28-29) and his healing ministry (15:31). The crowds marvel at Jesus' power and authority in healing (9:32-34; 12:22-24). Konradt proposes that here we see the crowds are on the way towards "recognizing the *unique and exceptional* nature of the divine care for Israel in Jesus" (2020, 221). The crowd's reaction during Jesus' entry into Jerusalem is also positive (21:8, 14-15). Third, Matthew distinguishes between the crowds and the disciples, with the former fulfilling the role of a "potential church." The crowd is instructed about John the Baptist (11:17-20) and invited to take up Jesus' yoke (11:28-30) but the disciples are those who are Jesus' siblings (12:46-50) and who are invited to take up their cross (16:24), since they are the ones who have insight into who Jesus really is (13:10-17).

Fourth, Konradt examines the crowds in 27:11-26. He notes that when Jesus enters Jerusalem, the crowd are not hostile, but by 27:25, they are before Pilate, taking responsibility for the death of Jesus. In Konradt's reading, both Pilate and the Jewish authorities attempt to use the crowd in order to get the result they hope for, whether that is Jesus' release or his crucifixion.

Konradt suggests Pilate thinks he has the crowd on his side, and that is why
he introduces the Passover amnesty, as a way of circumventing the chief
priests and elders. But it is the Jewish authorities who succeed in using the
crowd to get what they want. Konradt notes that the authorities
"persuaded" (27:20) the crowd and argues that

> the seduction of the people gathered before Pilate becomes
> paradigmatic for any instance of the authorities misleading their
> own people, and thus on the level of communication serves as a
> harsh warning against trusting the authorities (2020, 227).

Konradt sees no particular significance in the shift from "crowd" (27:15, 20,
24) to "all the people" (27:25), arguing it does not mean they represent all
Israel, but that they belong to Israel and their actions take place within
Israel, following the pattern of resistance to God's messengers that has
occurred throughout Israel's history. The particular focus is on the
inhabitants of Jerusalem (note the reference to "the whole city," 21:10, and
Jesus' comment on Jerusalem as the city that kills the prophets, 23:37). By
saying "his blood be upon us," the people take legal responsibility for Jesus'
death and since that is, in Matthew's view, innocent blood, they pay the
due penalty, in the form of the destruction of Jerusalem. The "children"
indicates the next generation, who suffered with their parents when the
Holy City was destroyed.

Konradt is clear that Matthew does not interpret the destruction of
Jerusalem as a judgement on Israel. Rather, it is a warning, a sign of God's
judgement on those who opposed Jesus, namely the Jewish authorities, and
those who were persuaded by the authorities, namely the crowd in
Jerusalem. This crowd is different from the crowds in Galilee and those
who accompanied him to Jerusalem. This latter group is representative of
those the Matthean community continues to reach out to with their
message of Jesus the Messiah. Konradt concludes that the Matthean
community is not a sect with clearly defined boundaries between
themselves and their Jewish peers. Rather it is a group with a nucleus of
core believers and a periphery of those who are more or less interested,
whose numbers fluctuate over time. Part of Matthew's reason for writing

is to attract those on the fringes of his group to make a firmer commitment. As Konradt explains, this call to commitment to Christ consists of at least three factors: the positive reaction of the crowds; the polemic against the Pharisees, who are blind guides; and the negative assessment of the Jewish authorities. All function both to stabilise the community and persuade those on the fringes to make a positive decision for membership of the Matthean community. The destruction of Jerusalem can also be interpreted to support this drive; it legitimates the followers of Jesus and disqualifies "the opposition in the community's conflict with the Pharisaic synagogue." The main aim is to ensure the crowds know who to trust and follow (2020, 231).

Konradt makes a useful point as to the importance of recognising that boundaries between groups are porous and fuzzy, not rigid and insurmountable. Whilst the aim of the rhetoric may be to enforce a clear distinction, the reality might be messier. But this raises a question – does Matthew intend 27:25 to force a choice? Is Matthew asking his audience, do you accept responsibility for Jesus' blood? And if so, in what way, as his killers, or through faith in him as saviour?

Matthew within Judaism

This section discusses the views of Saldarini, Kampen, Overman and Gale. The main aim of the Matthew within Judaism School is to limit the application of 27:25 to those present and their immediate descendants.

Anthony Saldarini

In his discussion of Matthew's use of "people," Saldarini examines 27:25 as a particular polemical case. Saldarini argues that the crowds at the Passover festival are initially sympathetic towards Jesus (21:8-10, 15, 46; 22:33) but they are subsequently manipulated by the Jerusalem religious leadership (chief priests, elders, scribes) and oppose Jesus (26:47, 55; 27:15-26). Saldarini disagrees with the interpretation of 27:25 as a sign of the rejection of Israel and the end of the Jewish mission. Rather, he notes that "crowd"

(27:15, 24), "crowds" (27:20) and "people" (27:25) are all synonyms for the same group. Saldarini argues that "people" is not used in a technical, theological sense in this verse. He acknowledges that "people" can indicate Jews ruled over by Jewish leaders (2:4; 21:23; 26:3, 47; 27:1) and it does mean the whole people of Israel at the start of the Gospel (1:21; 2:6; 4:16, 23). But in the trial scene, he argues, "people" indicates a sub-group, namely those who "are led away from Jesus by the institutional leaders of Israel" (1994, 32). This group cannot be the Jewish people throughout the Roman empire, or even Israel, but are those Jews in Jerusalem who support Jesus' execution. For Saldarini, "people" is used in 27:25 as an "ironic prophecy of judgement," namely the destruction of the temple in 70 CE, that they pronounce upon themselves (1994, 33). This means that for Matthew, the destruction of Jerusalem and the temple are divine punishment for the death of Jesus. This punishment is not aimed at all Jews for all time, but against those who were in Jerusalem, and their children, that is "those who were in Jerusalem when Jesus died and those of the next generation, who were alive about forty years after Jesus' death when Jerusalem was destroyed" (1994, 33). Saldarini finds a hint of this reading in Jesus' lament over Jerusalem (23:37-24:2). It is only by ignoring the narrative context that this verse can be understood as indicating a rejection of Israel as a whole.

Thus, for Saldarini, "all the people" (27:25) indicates Jerusalem and the leadership of the nation. This is part of Matthew's continuing attack on the leaders of Israel, including those who persecute the Matthean community. In order to do this, Matthew has substantially re-worked Mark's trial narrative, adding in the detail about Pilate's wife's dream and Pilate's own abdication of responsibility, in order to set up a sharp contrast with the Jewish leaders and their determination to have Jesus crucified. Saldarini reiterates his contention that Matthew is not indicating all Jews in his time or for all time, but the fate of Jerusalem and the opposition he and his community are experiencing from the leadership of the Jewish community. In Saldarini's reading of Matthew, both the disciples, the crowds and the people all remain somewhat ambiguous throughout the text; their responses to Jesus are mixed. Even the disciples still doubt as they are commissioned to share the good news (28:16-20), and the Jewish nation remains one of those needing to be won over by Jesus' teachings. Saldarini admits that Matthew was critical of his fellow Jews, but notes that so was Josephus. For both Matthew and Josephus, it was the Jewish religious authorities that were culpable for the destruction of Jerusalem and the chaos which followed (1994, 32-34). The condemnation of Matthew 27:25 is thus focused and specific to those gathered in Jerusalem at the moment of Jesus' trial, and their immediate descendants.

John Kampen

In his discussion of Jesus' trial and crucifixion (2019, 174-82) Kampen argues that it was the Romans who had the power to impose capital punishment, and that they used crucifixion as a public method of execution to deter opposition. There is, he suggests, little evidence of Jewish authorised capital punishment at this time. He gives examples of Pilate's oppressive approach to government, citing Josephus' accounts of the bringing of a bust of Emperor Tiberius on Roman military standards of troops based in Jerusalem, and of Pilate's plan to use temple funds to build an aqueduct to supply Jerusalem with water. The brutality and callousness of Pilate's actions are taken as evidence of the plausibility of the trial narrative.

Focusing specifically on 27:25, Kampen argues

> Responsibility for the death of Jesus has been shifted to the Jewish leadership by the author of the first gospel. In this account they are the ones charged with whipping up the crowds, who are portrayed as rather powerless pawns manipulated into taking responsibility for the death (2019, 177).

Kampen notes that Matthew widens the circle of responsibility to include the Pharisees and Sadducees. Kampen is sceptical that these groups bore historical responsibility, and argues their inclusion here is primarily because of Matthew's agenda to discredit his own opponents. Whilst Matthew may have his own agenda, it is clear that the Roman imperial system is primarily responsible for the death of Jesus, as seen by Pilate's order to set a guard on the tomb, which Kampen proposes was fulfilled by soldiers under Pilate's direct command. This raises the question of theological versus political responsibility, presuming these two can be distinguished. Whilst faith was integral to public life in the first-century, it is possible that Matthew holds the Roman authorities politically responsible for Jesus' death, but lays the theological blame squarely at the feet of the Jewish Jerusalem leadership.

When he discusses Pilate washing his hands, Kampen argues that Matthew's sectarian community distinguishes itself not from Rome, but from the rest of the Jewish community. Roman responsibility for the death of Jesus is denied, in the face of plain evidence to the contrary, and placed firmly on the shoulders of the Jewish leaders and the crowd who support them. The life of Matthew's community is understood by them as "a critique of how other Jewish people live out their religious devotion and of the views advocated by other Jewish leaders" (2020, 392). The facts are much less important than how they are interpreted.

J. Andrew Overman

Overman discusses the meaning of "council," or in Greek, *Sanhedrin*, in some detail. He explains that although it became a technical term for Rabbinic Judaism, in the first-century it did not refer to an official Jewish court. Rather, it indicated an imposition from the ruling Roman authorities, who divided Palestine up into administrative regions, each with their own council. Thus, any court or council referred to in the Gospels indicates a "thoroughly Roman judicial institution," consisting of both local elites and Roman officials assigned to the region. This means that although there was Jewish involvement, councils were Roman tools for controlling the local populace (1996, 372-73).

When he examines Jesus' trial before Pilate, Overman explains that Pilate is a minor figure in Matthew, whose primary function is to show that he, a Roman official, thought Jesus to be less of a threat than did the leaders of other local competing Judaisms (1996, 379). Overman argues that it is unlikely that Jesus was subject to the full weight of the Roman judicial system, but rather that "a few people with the right amount of influence in and around Jerusalem were able to get some Roman officials to lend their stamp of approval to dealing with Jesus definitively and expeditiously" (1996, 381). This is perfectly possible, but what difference does it make? If Overman is right, then perhaps the blame for Jesus' death can be narrowly applied to just a few people. But what place does this type of historical reconstruction have within theology? My concern here is not with the historicity of Matthew (although that is a valid and interesting question), but how his theology has been interpreted and used to justify pogroms and worse.

Overman begins his discussion of Matthew 27:25 by noting this verse has contributed more to the Christian charge of Jewish culpability in the death of Jesus than any other in the New Testament. Moreover, it has served to legitimate persecution of Jewish people simply for being Jewish. His exposition commences with an examination of texts related to the death of King Saul. Overman notes that 1 Samuel 26:11 and 2 Samuel 1:16 warn against killing the Lord's anointed, which in the Greek translation would be "killing the Lord's Christ" (*kyrios christos*). In the text from 2 Samuel, David says "Your blood be on your head; for your own mouth has testified against you, saying, 'I have killed the Lord's anointed.'" (NRSV). Overman then turns to 1 Maccabees, which refers to the shedding of innocent blood in reference to persecution of the Jewish people and the desecration of the temple (1 Maccabees 1:36-38). This would, of course, have resonated with a Jewish audience recovering from the destruction of the temple in 70 CE. Finally, Overman points out that when Judas displays remorse, he says he is guilty of betraying innocent blood (Matthew 27:4).

For Overman, Matthew 27:25 is a midrash on the themes identified above in Samuel and Maccabees. Matthew is arguing that yet again the Jewish leaders have killed God's chosen agent, and so are culpable and guilty before him. The addition of "and our children" is taken as a reference to the generation which witnessed the destruction of the temple. Thus, Matthew is providing a theodicy for an event which troubled all faithful Jews. "His explanation was fashioned for, and perhaps intelligible to, his community of Jesus-centred Jews" (1996, 383).

Overman is clear that responsibility stays with that generation. There is no sense that all Jews for all time are responsible for the death of Jesus, or that they owe some kind of cosmic debt for Jesus' death. Rather Matthew believed that corrupt local leaders, working together with the Roman authorities, arranged for Jesus to be killed, which ultimately resulted in Jerusalem being destroyed. But sadly, that is not how the text has been read throughout history.

Overman concludes his discussion of the passion narrative by asking two questions: why was Jesus killed and who killed him? Overman is clear that Jesus' death has, for centuries, been a pretext for Christian persecution and killing of Jews. But if this is a false reading of the narrative, what is an accurate one? Overman makes three preliminary points. First, that Jesus was a historical figure and the one event in his life we can be most confident actually took place is his crucifixion. Second, that Jesus was probably not subject to a full, detailed trial, but rather a quiet, behind-the-scenes, removal of an inconvenience. Third, the "council" was not an official court. It typically referred to a gathering of officials, possibly both Jewish and Roman, dealing with local issues. "Matthew's narrative betrays that in all likelihood the decision to get rid of Jesus was arrived at quickly by an impromptu gathering of local elders one evening" (1996, 385). This group then spoke with Roman officials, symbolised by Pilate, to arrange official Roman approval for their action. In Overman's reconstruction, this meeting would have recognised that Jesus' movement and message might not have posed a significant threat to peace and stability, but that it would be better to be sure, and so they agreed to have him executed on the understanding he was a rebel that needed dealing with. The title on Jesus' cross, "King of the Jews" is a further indication that he was seen as a potential threat to the security of the state.

Overman suggests there are incidents within Matthew's gospel that could have become the basis for this charge. There is, for example, his statement that he is greater than the temple (12:2), or the charge in the crucifixion scene that implied Jesus said he would destroy the temple (27:40). Added to this are the assertions, the Christological claims, that Jesus made about himself. Finally, there are his apocalyptic statements, that spoke of the end of the current political order and the incoming of a new age. Thus, Overman concludes, Jesus was killed by a coalition of local Jewish leaders and provincial Roman officials, because he was, or seemed to potentially be, a threat to public order and the status quo. One cannot say that "the Jews" killed Jesus, but rather that Jews and Gentiles, particularly those in political authority, did so because they believed it was politically expedient to act in this way (1996, 381-91). In this way Overman provides a useful and plausible reconstruction of the historical happenings surrounding Jesus' execution. But this does not address theological understandings of his death. A good historical understanding is an important foundation. But will it preach?

Aaron Gale

Gale's notes on Matthew in the *Annotated Jewish Study New Testament* include a brief panel on what he terms "the blood cry" of 27:25, which he explains has been used by some to argue that all Jews for all time were responsible for the death of Jesus. Gale states this claim may even date back to 1 Thessalonians 2:14-16, where Paul blames "the Jews" for the death of Jesus, although since Paul himself was Jewish it is likely the reference is primarily to the Jewish religious leadership. But the Church Fathers certainly held Jews in general responsible for the death of Jesus. Gale cites Justin Martyr as an example of this trend. For Gale, the more likely interpretation is that Matthew sees this as prophetic fulfilment of Jesus' predictions of the destruction of Jerusalem: it was "all the people" in the crowd, and their children, who saw the destruction of the temple in 70 CE (2017, 62). This is an important reminder that the charge of deicide is early and deeply rooted in Christian history.

Six evangelical views

R T France

In his theological overview, France is clear that Matthew's Gospel holds faith in Jesus as the Messiah to be the defining criterion by which one may join the people of God; ethnicity is no longer relevant. France laments what he regards as the misuse of 27:25 as the basis of Christian anti-Judaism. He discusses the attitude towards Judaism held by other New Testament authors, notably Paul, whose views range from dismissive (1 Thessalonians 2:14-16), to an elaborate scheme for the salvation of "all Israel" (Romans 9-11). France proposes that questions of definition are key. If by anti-Judaism, one means "the unbelief of the majority of the Jewish people has forfeited their privileged position as the unique people of God, that there is now a new basis of membership in the people of God based not on racial descent but on relationship with Jesus," then Matthew is indeed anti-Jewish (1989, 240). But this does not mean Matthew is against Jewish people. Far from it. Rather there is a continuing mission to the Jews, to bring them to a place of acceptance of Jesus as the Messiah. France does not think it at all anti-Jewish to record both Matthew's current failure to persuade the majority of Jews to join him, and his continuing enthusiasm for the furtherance of those efforts. That is to say, Matthew does not gloat over Jewish rejection of Jesus, nor does he want them to be punished for doing so. Rather he longs for them to be saved, and has written a gospel to encourage this, and also to warn the church lest they fail to learn from Israel's example (1989, 206-41). This is a useful distinction and a reminder of how many Christians interpret these texts.

France begins his discussion of Matthew 27:11-26 by describing this as the formal trial in which a guilty verdict that results in a sentence of execution can be delivered. France explains that Matthew puts "primary responsibility" for Jesus' death on the Jewish authorities and the people, but this does not mean Pilate is guiltless. The charge is framed in political terms, but Pilate is unconvinced, for three reasons: Jesus' silence under interrogation; his assessment that the Jewish leaders want to eliminate Jesus by any means possible; and the warning from his wife's dream. But even so, his "theatrical" attempts to absolve himself of responsibility will fool no one but Pilate himself. France recognises the terrible legacy of the blood cry of 27:25, arguing that the most appropriate response is to strive to understand accurately what Matthew meant by including this, discerning how it fits with Matthew's theology of fulfilment (2007, 1047-50).

When he discusses the shift of the crowd from supporting Jesus to calling for his death (Matthew 27:21-23), France proposes this was, at least in part, because Jesus was "officially judged a blasphemer by their recognised leaders; he is no longer an interesting novelty but a dangerous heretic" (2007, 1055). When "the Jews" say "his blood be upon us" (27:25), they are, France explains, taking "direct acceptance of responsibility" for Jesus' death. These are not merely the thoughtless words of a small gathering of hooligans, but that of the *laos*, the people, the same word that is used within the Septuagint to indicate God's chosen people. The reference to "and our children" further extends the scope of the reference. France recognises this phrase is problematic for contemporary Christians, but argues we must first determine what Matthew meant by it. France states that Matthew meant more than simply those in front of Pilate's palace that morning. He takes the reference to "our children" as indicating the generation that bore the brunt of the Roman assault on Jerusalem in 70 CE. But the wider shift is theological. He explains:

> The kingdom of heaven is no longer to be focused in the *laos*, the city and the temple, but in the vindicated and enthroned Son of Man who, after the temple is destroyed, will gather his chosen people from all the corners of the earth (2007, 1058).

All this would happen within a generation (hence the reference to "us and our children"). Thus, the reference is primarily theological, focused on the establishment of the new people of God, not on condemnation of Jewish people simply because they are Jewish (2007, 1056-58). In France's interpretation, the reference is broad, but not ethnically focused. The dichotomy is no longer Jew and gentile; the new distinction is between Christ-follower and Christ-rejector.

Donald Hagner

In his overview of the passion narrative, Hagner argues that there is a strong sense of irony: "Though sinful men do their best to thwart the mission of Jesus, they accomplish the very purpose for which he came and thus fulfil God's will." Hagner has a nuanced position on the historicity of the narrative at this point. He is certain that there is a historical core to what is recorded here, but at the same time, he argues that Matthew has been creative in how he recounts events. That is not to say anything is made up, but rather to recognise that a degree of artistic license has been deployed in how the facts are retold (1995, 750).

On Judas, his betrayal of Jesus and subsequent remorse, Hagner is clear that Judas and the Jewish priests act freely, from their own motivation, as unwitting instruments used to accomplish God's purposes. They represent only themselves, not Jews or Judaism (1995, 816). When he discusses Pilate's decision to free Barabbas, Hagner is clear that although it is not attested outside the Gospels, that does not mean there is no historical basis for the custom. Moreover, Pilate does not escape responsibility for Jesus' death simply because he washes his hands (1995, 822-24).

Hagner explains that the idea of blood being "upon someone" or "upon their head" is found in the Hebrew scriptures (for example 2 Samuel 1:16; Jeremiah 26:15) and in the New Testament (Acts 5:28; 18:6). The reference to children is one of familial solidarity (as, for example, in Joshua 7:24; 2 Kings 24:3-4 or Jeremiah 31:29; Ezekiel 18:2). He adds

> A proper understanding of this text, however, must begin with the realization that those demanding Jesus' death are primarily the Jewish leaders or at most the particular crowds whipped up by them. It is certainly only the Jews of that generation – and indeed, only *some* of them – who are responsible for the death of Jesus (1995, 827).

In Hagner's understanding, Matthew could well see that judgement did fall on that generation (and their children) when Jerusalem was destroyed. But this does not mean that Christians are encouraged to bring vengeance on Jewish people. There is clear teaching that vengeance belongs to the Lord (Deuteronomy 32:35; Romans 12:19; Hebrews 10:30), and Jesus teaches Christians to love everyone, including their enemies (Matthew 5:44; Romans 12:19-21) (1995, 827). This is an important limitation of application of the verse, especially the refusal to allow Christians to judge or condemn.

Hagner recognises that subsequent interpreters might read the blood of Jesus in a redemptive or salvific sense, but argues it is anachronistic to read this sense into this verse. Hagner concludes that theologically there is only one cause of the death of Jesus: human sinfulness, which afflicts us all. "The crucifixion is in this sense a piece of the autobiography of every man and woman ever to walk this earth. It is 'I' who am guilty of crucifying Jesus" he concludes (1995, 827-28). This is the key evangelical Christian move; Jesus may have chosen his own death but it remains my responsibility, as it deals with my sin.

Craig Keener

Keener begins his discussion of Jesus' arrest and trial with a long excursus explaining why there is a historical core to the passion narratives (1999, 607-11). Keener also discusses the nature of the *Sanhedrin*, which he describes as a ruling council. He argues for it being a more structured body than Overman's proposal. For Keener, the *Sanhedrin* was "the municipal aristocracy of Jerusalem," which had national influence, as far as the Roman prefects and Herodian princes allowed them to (1999, 615). If this reconstruction is correct, it was the national elite who acted through official channels to arrange for Jesus to be executed.

Keener argues for the historicity of the trial narratives, explaining that sources such as Joseph of Arimathea (Mark 15:43), those connected to the High Priest's household (John 18:15-16) or even Jesus himself (Acts 1:3) provided the detail. He proposes that the cleansing of the temple offended the Sadducees and that while Jesus was arrested by the priestly authorities, but then executed by the Romans, the main opposition to the followers of Jesus came from the priests. He adds that whilst those with antisemitic motivation abuse this text to blame the entirety of the Jewish people, the reality is that the responsibility lies with the Jewish political elite, a group that other Jews also complained about (1999, 644-46).

In Keener's reading of the trial narrative, the guilt for Jesus' death rests partly on Pilate, but also on "the insistent people, blindly following their religious leaders" who take upon themselves the moral responsibility for

Jesus' death. Indeed, motivated by the conflict with the Jewish leaders of his own day, Matthew appears to place more responsibility for Jesus' death on his own people than on Pilate. Keener adds that washing hands "most obviously constituted a repudiation of responsibility for innocent blood in Jewish tradition," citing Deuteronomy 21:6-7; Psalm 26:6 and Isaiah 1:15-16 in support (1999, 662). Formal, legal responsibility for Jesus' death remains with Pilate; Keener proposes Pilate chose political expediency over justice, but that in Matthew's telling, it is the Jewish leaders who incur the greater guilt for it is they who continually insisted on capital punishment (1996, 662-65).

Turning to 27:25, Keener suggests the crowd represents the ambivalence of God's people, who are swayed by different competing voices. Whilst he recognises subsequent interpreters have read other meanings into the blood cry, seeing both an offer of salvation through the blood of atonement and an irrevocable, everlasting curse, Keener argues that for Matthew, "the curse invoked in this verse was fulfilled in the year 70, 'children' in this instance referring to the generation immediately following from that multitude" (1999, 671). This is an intriguing interpretation; does Keener's limitation of the scope of Matthew 27:25 also limit the scope of the offer of salvation? What is clear is that for Keener, responsibility for Jesus' death is shared, a move also made by Nolland.

John Nolland

Nolland discusses Jesus' trial before Pilate in two sections (27:11-14 and 27:15-26). I will focus only on the second of these. For Nolland, Pilate is not spared responsibility for the death of Jesus, and any attempt to read Matthew as implying the Jews are solely responsible is a mis-reading of the text.

The pardoning of Jesus Barabbas and the condemnation of Jesus of Nazareth could, Nolland proposes, have some basis in history. Whether there was a general custom of a paschal pardon, or whether it was simply that Barabbas was, in Pilate's view, worthy of no more than a flogging is a moot point. What is clear from the text is that in relation to the fate of Jesus of Nazareth, Pilate equivocates, keeps his own counsel and eventually hands Jesus over for crucifixion without ever formally pronouncing a guilty verdict. The crowd's shift from supporting Jesus in earlier chapters to now calling for his death is attributed, in Nolland's view, to nationalism. Barabbas was a glamourous freedom fighter and the obvious choice of the leaders of the Jewish people; hence the crowd backed him. They even begin to threaten to riot, in order to bring an end to Pilate's prevarication. Pilate, sensing he has no choice, washes his hands as a claim of innocence, a kind of prophylactic against guilt, before handing Jesus over to the verdict of the crowd and to crucifixion (2005, 1166-78).

Nolland suggests 27:25 should be read as "a statement of readiness to take responsibility, not a confession of guilt." The reference to "on our children" is not a decision to pass guilt down the generations, but a recognition that the judgement will fall within a generation, hence it will impact the children of those present (2005, 1178). Nolland adds

> By this stage in Matthew's story the landscape is littered with people who share responsibility for Jesus' death. Some, like Judas and the people, readily own responsibility; some, like the chief priests and the elders, prefer to see the responsibility fall elsewhere; and some, like the disciples and especially Peter, simply deny and abandon Jesus. All are guilty (2005, 1178).

Nolland adds that the death of Jesus on a cross both reveals the guilt of all, but also offers forgiveness to all people. He is unpersuaded by the reading that sees blood poured out for forgiveness in this verse and so rejects the redemptive reading of this particular verse. But overall, Nolland is typical of evangelical interpreters in broadening the moral responsibility for the death of Jesus to include everyone (2005, 1179).

Tom Wright

Wright introduces some of the characters in the passion narrative:

Here are the chief priests and elders. For them, the death of Jesus is a political necessity. He has challenged their power, he's captured the crowd's imagination, and he can't be allowed to get away with it. They don't suppose for a minute he might be a true prophet, let alone Israel's Messiah. Their naked political goals, unadorned with any desire for true justice, are a constant feature of the story. Do you know anyone like that? Have you ever seen them in the mirror? (2002b, 148).

The last two sentences are crucial. For Wright this is about "you and me" (that is, all Christians), not about "the Jews."

Wright suggests that when Jesus is on trial before Caiaphas, what is recorded are two "different ways of seeing and describing the whole world" (2002b, 167). Caiaphas understood himself, as High Priest, to have supreme authority over the temple, centred on the *realpolitik* of keeping peace with Rome, ensuring the people were happy and trouble-makers were kept away. Jesus, by contrast, was introducing a different world, one where people encountered healing, forgiveness and divine love and compassion, things they thought only possible in the Temple or through study of the Torah. For Jesus, the Jerusalem temple was a symbol of Israel's mistake in turning away from God. Since he could not explain this in a way that Caiaphas would hear, Jesus chose to remain silent (2002b, 167-68).

In his discussion of Jesus' trial before Pilate, Wright is clear that "Barabbas represents all of us. When Jesus dies, the brigand goes free, the sinners go free, we all go free" (2002b, 178). Wright is clear that in Matthew's account, all are guilty: Pilate, the chief priests and elders, the crowds. Wright alludes to the cry of the crowd in 27:25, but describes their children as those "who would grow up to be the next generation of brigands, to be cut down or crucified in their thousands by Pilate's heirs and successors as Jerusalem lurched towards its final downfall" (2002b, 179). There is no explicit discussion of the blood cry, but there is an implicit rejection of the antisemitic reading of it, for in Wright's understanding of the passage, we cannot say "the Jews killed Jesus," but rather "we all killed Jesus." This point is underlined in his discussion of the crucifixion itself, where he explains that Matthew has written it so we can put ourselves in the story, ensuring that we worship "this Jesus in whose death we see the face of God turned towards us in love" (2002b, 184).

Martin Goldsmith

In his discussion of Jesus' trial, Goldsmith notes that the Jewish leaders levelled two accusations against Jesus: of claiming superiority to the temple (26:61) and of claiming to be the Messiah, the Son of God (26:63). That is to say, he was accused of blasphemy and a shocking disrespect for the temple. In Goldsmith's reading of the text, there follows an unjust and illegal mockery of a trial (2001, 186).

> Pilate washes his hands in a pathetic attempt to rid himself of guilt, but history has shown the futility of such hand-washing. The Christian creeds have declared throughout the centuries that Jesus "suffered under Pontius Pilate". On the other hand, the thoughtlessly bold exclamation of the Jewish crowds "let his blood be upon us and on our children" has had tragic consequences too. Christians throughout the ages have persecuted Jews as "Christ killers," ignoring the fact that he was killed by the Romans, the combined forces of the various movements of the Jewish leadership and at the insistence of the crowds. All joined together in mutual guilt, both Jews and Gentiles of all strata of society. So Paul declares that "Jews and Gentiles alike are all under sin" (Rom 3.9) before going on to show that justification comes to both Jew and Gentile through the atoning work of Jesus on the cross (Rom 3:21-31) (2001, 187).

Goldsmith finds a clear contrast between Peter's bitter weeping and repentance, and Judas' suicide. Both fail Jesus, both are guilty before him; but while one repents and is restored, the other does not see any possibility of change and so kills himself. Goldsmith presumes that the crowd did gather to call for Jesus' death and for Barabbas to be released. He speculates that the crowd might have been hoping for a political or military messiah, and when that desire was frustrated, they rejected Jesus, including rejecting

"God's chosen way of salvation through the suffering of the cross" (2001, 189). Once again, Goldsmith shows how a popular evangelical exposition of a complex and controversial passage can explicitly reject antisemitism.

Discussion and conclusions

As the discussion above has shown, the best way of interpreting 27:25 is to limit the potential scope of application; whilst in a theological sense, Christians may want to argue that all bear responsibility for the death of Christ, the cry of blood guilt must be restricted to those in the crowd and their immediate descendants. Any possibility of a more general application must be rejected out of hand. This move is made by virtually all the interpreters discussed in this chapter. Interestingly, the evangelical interpreters also, in the main, rejected the salvific reading of 27:25, seeing no reference to implicit salvation in the verse. The outliers are perhaps Heil and Sider-Hamilton. They both, in different ways, include more Jewish people in their interpretation; the former by implying culpability, and the latter by presuming (unwitting) salvation. Is either approach acceptable? I remain to be fully convinced that they are.

Scholars of the New Testament will always argue over how historically accurate Matthew's trial scene is. It is impossible to achieve certainty, and in a way such arguments miss the point, for Matthew was not writing history, but theology. There is merit in Bauckham's point, discussed above, about the gospels as eyewitness testimony, but even so, the emphasis is on testimony, that is, the account of a believer as to what happened and *what it means*. In the case of Matthew 27:25, the argument of this chapter is that the acceptance of responsibility of blood guilt is very limited and has no universal or broad-reaching application.

The Matthew within Judaism school are at pains to point out that any reading of Matthew 27:25 must limit the scope of application to those present and their immediate descendants. In this reading, Jerusalem and her inhabitants are regarded as being punished for the death of Jesus, but that punishment is now complete and there is no valid reason to extend it further. This point should be held in tension with the evangelical desire to recognise both the universal need of salvation and the universal offer of salvation that is found in the death of Christ. None of the scholars discussed above wishes to promote an antisemitic reading of Matthew's Gospel, but their motivations and methods differ. The task of this book is to provide possibilities for preachers today to continue to teach Christianity faithfully without being heard as potentially antisemitic. Before we do this, we will turn to discuss the blood libel, an egregious stain on the history of the church.

Chapter 6
From Blood Cry to Blood Libel

The main focus of this chapter is to outline some of the antisemitic views held by some Christians in the period between when Matthew's Gospel was written right up to the present day. This is, of course, a complex topic that could be discussed at far greater length than has been allocated to it here (but see Chazan 2016, Gerdmar 2009, Lipton 2014, Ruether 1997 amongst others). The purpose of the brief overview here is merely to note that anti-Jewish readings of Matthew's Gospel provided the conditions in which antisemitism flourished. That antisemitism often resulted in violence against Jews, including their deaths. Christian preachers and teachers have a duty to understand this reality, and to keep it in mind as they preach and teach.

As the previous chapters of this book have demonstrated, the first (Jewish) followers of Jesus struggled to find their place in society and understandably felt under threat for their lives. They responded with polemic, a tendency that was continued by the (gentile) followers of Jesus who came after them. This is the so-called *Adversus Judaeos* tradition, which is arguably based, at least in part, on the assumption of Jewish culpability for the death of Jesus. For example, the third-century African Father Cyprian wrote three volumes against the Jews, stating they were subject to God's wrath for idolatry, disbelieving and killing the prophets, failing to understand the scriptures, that they would lose Jerusalem and much more in this vein (Ruether 1997, 118). In his history of the church, Eusebius is negative about the Jews and portrays the destruction of Jerusalem as the Jews suffering the consequences of their betrayal of Jesus, although it should be noted that Eusebius portrays the Roman authorities and various heretics as other problems for the church (Chazan 2016, 51-52). Similarly, in his sermons, John Chrysostom of Antioch condemned the Jews as legalists, whose religious observances were all pointless following the destruction of Jerusalem (Wilken 1983, 148-58). This negative rhetoric continued down the centuries, but did become more sophisticated over time. As Chazan explains, the Church Father Augustine "provided a highly nuanced view of Jewish past, present and future" (2016, 21).

Chazan cites Jeremy Cohen's distillation of six key elements to Augustine's thought. First, that the survival of Jewish people scattered in exile across the world was evidence of their punishment for rejecting and crucifying Jesus. Second, Jewish failure to recognise Jesus as Messiah fulfilled biblical descriptions of their repudiation and replacement. Third, because Jewish people preserve the Old Testament, and use it wherever they live, this proves that Christians did not make up the prophecies found within the Old Testament about Jesus. Fourth, Jewish continued compliance with biblical law is a further corroborating testimony to the truth of Christianity. Fifth, the words of Psalm 59:12, "Slay them not, lest at any time they forget your law; scatter them in your might" are a prophetic statement of how Jews are to be treated in Christendom (that is, dispersed, dominated, demeaned, but not destroyed utterly). Sixth, refutation of Judaism contributes to the vindication of Christianity (Chazan 2016, 79-80).

There are clear links between Augustine's teaching and the blood cry with its associated charge of deicide that is rooted in Matthew 27:25. Augustine's first and second points are a direct extrapolation of this teaching, and the fifth is a logical consequence of belief that Jewish people are damned but it is for God to punish them in his chosen way according to his chosen agenda. In Augustine's view, Christianity therefore needed a weak Judaism, in order to justify its own existence and bolster its own position. This uneasy process of toleration and contempt for Jewish people continued for centuries, with Jewish people occupying marginal positions within society. Sadly, attitudes hardened over time and in the twelfth century shifted to a more violent attitude, as documented below. That is not to say all relationships between Christians and Jews were universally terrible. I have elsewhere documented some of the positive relationships that existed between Jewish people and Christians, and will not repeat those observations here (Wilson 2020, 21-25). The focus of the chapter is on noting the reality of the blood libel and arguing that whilst the deicide interpretation of Matthew 27:25 was not directly cited when the charges of ritual murder were levelled, it nevertheless formed an essential foundation for believing that Jewish people were capable of such actions.

An overview of the blood libel

The blood libel is the charge that Jewish people kill Christians, often Christian children, and drain their blood in order to make matzah for Passover. Whilst this whole charge is unbelievable for anyone with even the slightest knowledge of Judaism, perhaps the most difficult aspect to comprehend is the fact that while the blood libel has never been proved in court it has nevertheless persisted for centuries. E M Rose explains that most blood libel charges were never formally investigated, and where they were, torture was invariably employed to extract confessions from the Jews who were accused. Moreover, Christian emperors, kings, and popes all spoke out against blood libels, as did at least one Turkish sultan, not to mention Jews and Jewish converts to Christianity. But despite this history, despite the fact that no alleged victim of ritual murder remains in the Roman Catholic calendar of saints, the blood libel accusation remains and resurfaces, even up to the present day (Rose, 2015, 1). Thus, the blood libel can be considered a pernicious rumour, never proved, but long present, which had traction, at least in part, because of how Matthew 27:25 has been handled in Christian teaching and preaching.

Rose notes that the blood libel is difficult to categorise or explain. Some scholars have argued it is a hangover from antiquity, a development of Roman attacks on Christianity. Others have tried to establish links with Jewish practices such as circumcision or kosher butchering, or Jewish holiday food such as matzah, or the martyrdoms of the first crusade. Perhaps Christian doubts over their own beliefs or a desire to deal with a Jew to whom money was owed also played their part. Whatever the origins, the effect has been long-lasting. Although the blood libel is often written off as a medieval abrogation, the reality is that there were more accusations in the period between 1870 and 1935 than in all the previous centuries combined. The circumstances of each claim were unique, influenced by a variety of factors, such that whilst a generalised framework is possible, it loses the historicity of each situation if deployed carelessly. Rose's own focus is on William of Norwich as a specific exemplar of this horrific phenomenon (2015, 10-11).

Teter explains the circumstances around William's death:

> In 1144, during a bloody civil war in England, a twelve-year-old boy named William disappeared during the Easter season; his body was found on Good Friday by a forester in the Thorpe Wood near the town of Norwich, but was left there until Monday, after the holiday. On that day, the forester returned to bury it on the spot. Miracles were said to have followed, and William's body was moved to the monks' cemetery, then to a new sarcophagus in the chapter house, and finally to the cathedral. The Jews of Norwich were never tried or harmed as a result of William's death, though rumors apparently circulated soon thereafter. The lack of immediate action in response to the boy's death suggests that it was not treated as a martyr's death and that Jews were not seriously implicated. But the story is shrouded in mystery, because no contemporary record of any investigation exists (2020, 18).

A monk, Thomas of Monmouth, arrived in Norwich in the 1150s, and began to write a hagiographic account of William's death, which was completed between 1172 and 1174. Jews had only recently begun to live in Norwich; this was part of the reason for accusing them, but Teter argues that an increase in Christian piety that focused on Jesus' suffering as a human being was the root cause. In Thomas' retelling, William represented any Christian, or indeed Christ himself, "whom Jews killed out of hatred." Indeed, the tale Thomas wove drew heavily on the passion narrative for both symbolism and detail (Teter 2020, 18-19). An extract of Thomas' account will illustrate:

> And so, while the enemies of the Christian name ran riot around the boy in such a spirit of evil, there were others among them who, in mockery of the Passion of the Cross, sentenced him to be crucified. Once they did so they said: 'Just as we have condemned Christ to a most shameful death, so we condemn a Christian, so that we punish

both the Lord and his servant in the punishment of reproach; that which they ascribe to us we will inflict on them.' And so, conspiring to execute such execrable malice, they next seized the innocent victim with bloody hands and raised him from the ground. He was put upon the cross and they competed among themselves in rivalry to kill him (Rubin 2014, 17).

In a footnote on the quoted speech, "Just as we have condemned...", Rubin suggests there may be echoes of the Reproaches in the Good Friday liturgy, in which Christ remonstrates with his people. This theological tradition has at least some basis in the blood cry of Matthew 27:25.

Rose reconstructs the circumstances which led to the charges related to the murder of William. A core part of the argument is that the charge of ritual murder was used as a distraction technique during the trial of a knight, Simon de Novers. Rose recounts the failures of the Second Crusade, where many English knights borrowed considerable sums of money to fund their overseas adventures, in the hope of securing riches and success in the Holy Land. This did not come about, and many returned to England heavily indebted. Simon de Novers was one such knight, who owed a considerable sum to a Jewish man, most probably called Deulesalt. Rose explains that Duelesalt was probably the richest Jew living in Norwich at the time; he arrived in 1144, and lent money to many in the town. Simon, lacking the funds (and perhaps the desire) to repay Duelesalt, killed him in 1149. The Jews of the town appealed to King Stephen for justice, and a trial was arranged in London. Simon was defended by the Bishop of Norwich, William Turbe, who saw this as an opportunity to raise his own profile, as well as securing the future of his client. Bishop Turbe accused Deulesalt of being the ring leader in a Jewish plot to capture, torture and ritually kill the boy William, citing Jewish desire to inflict on him all the tortures that were inflicted on Jesus. Bishop Turbe constructed a conspiracy theory that a significant leader in the town, Aelward, and the Sheriff John de Chesney, were complicit in hiding the reality of the crime, as they were in the pay of the Jews.

The case suddenly became a complex one, and ended with Simon being released because the king could not determine his guilt or the facts related to the death of the boy William. King Stephen and his court did not denounce the blood libel, but nor did they find Duelesalt guilty of it. There were no immediate attacks on Jewish people in Norwich as a result of the trial, but the foundations had been laid. Thomas of Monmouth, together with Bishop Turbe, created the cult of St William that was a crucial precursor to other blood libels (Rose 2015, 75-91).

Rose argues that a particularly damaging feature of Thomas of Monmouth's accusation is that it "assigns guilt for an alleged murder of a Christian youth to the Jews as a people, rather than to individual perpetrators." Rose adds that later accounts developed an assertion "that Jews organized such murders in mockery of Christ and the Christian religion, and did so regularly and in different locales." This notion of collective blame is particularly damaging, as it paved the way for subsequent accusations against and condemnations of the Jewish people. A second key development occurred in Blois, where the Jews held responsible for murder of a child were condemned to be burnt to death. This overturned the previous approach of tolerating the Jews in the expectation that they would convert at the end of time. In Paris, Jews were expelled. Thus, through these and other incidents, the precedent was set: expulsion or elimination, choices that were enacted with devastating consequences in subsequent centuries (2015, 237).

Teter agrees that there are all kinds of problems with assuming William was a saint and martyr; Thomas' account is full of rebuttals of doubts about the conspiracy and cover up of William's murder by the Jews, as well as William himself, who was "rather questionable material for a saint," from a commoner background, with no reputation for piety or devotion (2020, 21).

Teter argues that the medieval charges of blood libel can be bookended by the accusations in Norwich and Trent. She explains the circumstances of the latter charge as follows:

During the Christian Holy Week of 1475, which started with Palm Sunday on March 19 and ended on Easter Sunday, March 26, rumors began circulating in Trent, a city at the foothills of the Alps, that Jews had killed a toddler named Simon. The boy disappeared on Thursday, March 23, while the tiny Jewish community of Trent was celebrating Passover, which had begun the evening before. Simon's body was discovered on Easter Sunday in a canal running under the house owned by a Jewish family. His death unleashed a chain of events that resulted in the destruction of Trent's tiny Jewish community and the creation of the cult of Little Simon, or Simonino as he would be called in Trent, with the relics of the boy's body at its center (2020, 43).

A fabricated account of Simon's ritual murder was extracted under torture from the Jews of Trent. The accuracy of the trial accounts was subsequently challenged; Jews from across the region mobilised to defend their peers. Teter documents how accounts of the Trent trial spread across Europe and recounts the development of the cult of Little Simon, as well as those Christians – including Popes – who resisted the scapegoating of the Jews more generally.

Whilst the accusations of ritual murder that formed the blood libel first surfaced in the twelfth century, it was not until the nineteenth and twentieth centuries that they became widespread. Previously, such charges had been mainly local in origin and impact, confined to obscure medieval chronicles. But now a local accusation could quickly spread and become part of "authoritative" accounts of world history, becoming indisputable "facts." Unsubstantiated rumours created patterns and concepts with which to describe Jewish people. Tales of earlier trials were used in subsequent events; those new trials were then cited in later events, and so a self-perpetuating chain of lies was promulgated, which remained unchallenged, even if also unproven, until the end of the eighteenth century (Teter 2020, 377). Counter-efforts did begin with Trent. Teter documents the efforts by some in leadership within the church, including some popes, to condemn blood libels, but notes it was not well publicised and not terribly effective, and that even though Jews turned to Christians for defence and support, they did not necessarily find the aid they hoped for. A picture emerges of Christians who are reluctant to defend Jews, perhaps in part because the teaching they have heard on Matthew 27:25 implies that all Jews everywhere are guilty of killing Christ.

Whilst it is tempting to think of blood libels as something of the distant, medieval past, this is not the case. In what follows I briefly note three more recent examples of blood libels before concluding that sadly this pernicious and destructive rumour is still alive and active today.

Ronald Florence on Damascus

Florence (2004) discusses the blood libel of 1840 in Damascus. Father Thomas, a Capuchin monk who had lived in Damascus for thirty-two years, went missing, together with his servant Ibrahim Amara, on the evening of Thursday 6th February 1840. No trace of either man was ever found. There is no evidence that the monastery in which they lived was robbed. Those investigating their disappearance found food ready to be cooked, and all their clothes and valuables undisturbed. A rumour spread that Father Thomas had been ritually murdered by Jews; the last sighting of him was him going into the Jewish quarter of Damascus on Wednesday 5th February 1840.

Since Father Thomas was under the protection of the French King, it was left to the French Consul, Ratti-Menton, a known antisemite, to investigate. He accused some of the leading Jewish figures in the city of ritual murder, linking it to the accusation Jews killed Christians to drain their blood and make matzah. Some of those arrested confessed to the murder under torture. There were subsequent violent attacks on Jews in the city, orchestrated by Christian and Muslim groups. This violence drew international attention, and under pressure from abroad the governor of Damascus released those Jews who were still imprisoned. In November 1840, when the Ottoman Empire re-established control over Damascus, all accusations of blood libel were dropped.

The "Damascus Affair" shattered the peaceful relationship that had existed between the Jewish and Christian minorities in Damascus. Moreover, it was the catalyst for a wave of blood libel accusations across Palestine,

Egypt, and Iran, amongst other Middle Eastern countries, in the forty years that followed. It also revived the blood libel myth in Europe, and is arguably related to subsequent blood libel accusations in both the Russian Empire and the USA.

Edmund Levin on Tsarist Russia

Levin discusses the case of a blood libel charge in Tsarist Russia. He explains the circumstances:

> In the spring of 1911, a young boy was found stabbed to death in a cave on the desolate outskirts of the city of Kiev, then part of the Russian Empire, his body riddled with some fifty puncture wounds. Four months later, a troop of police and gendarmes raided the home of a Jewish brick factory clerk named Mendel Beilis and dragged him off to prison in the middle of the night. Beilis's trail for the murder of thirteen-year-old Andrei Yushchinsky, which took place in the fall of 1913, was the most sensational court case of its time and surely one of the most bizarre ever tried in an ostensibly civilized society. The case was front-page news around the world. The reason for the intense international attention: the Russian state had charged Beilis not simply with the boy's murder but with the ritual Jewish killing of this Christian child (2014, xi).

Levin is clear that Beilis was an "improbable candidate" for such a murder that was claimed to be motivated by Jewish identity. Beilis was not an observant Jew and had very little religious learning. But that did not stop a Russian antisemitic group, the Black Hundreds, from blaming him, circulating a pamphlet at Andrei's funeral, which Levin reproduces in full:

> Orthodox Christians! The Yids have tortured Andrusha Yushchinsky to death! Every year, before their Passover, they torture to death several dozens of Christian children in order to get their blood to mix with their matzo. They do this to commemorate the suffering of our Saviour, whom they tortured to death on the cross. The official doctors found that before the Yids tortured Yushchinsky, they stripped him

naked, tied him up, stabbing him in the principal veins so as to get as much blood as possible. They pierced him in fifty places. Russians! If your children are dear to you, beat the Yids. Beat them up until there is not a single Yid left in Russia. Have pity on your children! Avenge the unfortunate martyr. It is time! It is time! (2014, 13)

Although there is no explicit mention of the blood cry of Matthew 27:25, and therefore no direct connection can be claimed, it is notable that the charge of deicide is levelled. This charge was, of course, rooted at least in part on a universalistic reading of Matthew 27:25, holding all Jews for all time responsible for the death of Jesus. This understanding of the blood cry as a root cause of the blood libel is reflected in Bernard Malamud's novel *The Fixer*, about the Kiev blood libel. He paints a picture of Beilis being subject to systematic antisemitic abuse because he is believed to be a "Christ killer" who was capable of the most unspeakable acts.

The case of Andrei's murder quickly became notorious. The overwhelming majority of outside observers regarded it as a stich up. Even some within Russia, including prominent Christians, sought to defend Beilis. Levin suggests that Andrei experienced domestic violence. Andrei's mother Alexandra often beat him; he would run to his aunt Natalia for protection. She believed it was his mother and step-father might have murdered him (his own father having abandoned his mother when she was pregnant with him). But the couple were cleared by the police, and there was no evidence to suggest they were the killers (2014, 19-21). Levin's argument is that Vera Cheberyak, a notorious local criminal, and her family / gang framed Beilis for the murder. Vera was accused by the defence, Beilis by the prosecution. Beilis was eventually acquitted by the jury. It has never been proved who murdered Andrei, but Levin's belief is that it was Vera Cheberyak and her family.

Edward Berenson on Massena, New York

The case that Berenson discusses is the disappearance of four-year-old Barbara Griffiths in the woods surrounding Massena, New York on Saturday 22nd September 1928. What is particularly odd about this case is that whilst the blood libel was present in Europe, it was largely absent in the US at the time. Massena had a tiny Jewish community, about twenty-five families, all from Eastern Europe (what is now Poland, Lithuania and Belarus), all of whom spoke the same dialect of Yiddish, ate the same food and had the same Orthodox practices and beliefs (2019, 26). This small, tight-knit community, was a potentially easy target for someone looking to stir up trouble.

Those searching for Barbara decided at some point on the night of 22nd September that this was a case of Jewish ritual murder. It is unclear why, but Berenson suggests that perhaps it came from Ku Klux Klan members or a recent migrant to the town. There were many Canadian migrants in the town, and blood libel stories were more present in Canada than the US at that time. Other factors may also have been in play.

Berenson notes that autumn 1928 was the time for campaigning in the presidential election, which pitted the Protestant, Republican, Herbert Hoover against the Catholic, Democrat, Al Smith. Smith was popular in urban areas and amongst recent migrants, including Jews, whilst Hoover resonated more with rural, socially conservative longer-term residents. The campaign was polemical and brutal, with supporters of the Republican candidate (although not Hoover himself) stirring up anti-Catholic, anti-immigrant and antisemitic sentiments. This included the Ku Klux Klan, who were active in Massena, including in sharing antisemitic conspiracies. Berenson notes that it is probable that the overwhelming majority of eligible voters in Massena would have voted Republican. It is therefore plausible to presume many residents were at least open to the possibility that there was truth in an antisemitic rumour that Barbara was kidnapped by Jews who intended to ritually murder her (2019, 153-76).

But whatever the cause, a blood libel accusation began to circulate. Barbara was found alive and well at about 4:30 on the Sunday afternoon, in a farmer's field less than a mile from her house. Having failed to find her brother and after getting lost, she'd ended up sleeping outside (2019, 181-83). Unfortunately, the fact that Barbara was found safe and well did not end the problem for the town's Jews. Instead, a new rumour circulated that they decided to let her go once they realised the strength of feeling amongst the people. Barbara's mother fled the town to get some peace from the press; Barbara was known for the next few decades as "the girl who got lost in the woods" (2019, 183).

The blood libel remained an issue in the press, especially as Massena's Jews sought justice and an apology from the town's mayor and state trooper who had first believed and acted upon the accusation. The key point to note from this incident is that although the story became a press sensation, there was no sense that the accusation was believable amongst the US press. Thus, whilst blood libels appeared credible in medieval Europe, they had no standing in twentieth century USA. But that does not mean the charge of deicide or the accusation of ritual murder had been quashed. Far from it.

Conclusion: the responsibility of the church

This chapter has traced the development and spread of the blood libel down the centuries. Although it cannot be proven, one of the assumptions of this chapter is that the deicide focused interpretation of Matthew 27:25 was foundational to the plausibility of the blood libel. If it was believed that "the Jews killed Jesus" and moreover that they accepted responsibility for his death, it was only a small step to believing "the Jews" were persecuting and killing Christians for their own purposes. None of the accusations discussed above had any real basis in fact. Yet they all did immense damage. Christians are sadly ignorant of this history, which perhaps explains why blood libels and Christian antisemitism persist to this day.

In his conclusion, Berenson discusses the Polish post-war pogroms which saw Holocaust survivors murdered when they returned to their own towns (2019, 206-10). Berenson also provides evidence of anti-Jewish sentiment and pogroms in the Soviet Union, even in the Russian Orthodox Church (2019, 211-14). He discusses a recent Italian historian's book *Passovers of Blood*, which also promulgates the blood libel (2019, 215-20), as well as a recent sermon in Al Aqsa in Jerusalem, the third holiest site in Islam:

In June 2015, Sheikh Kalel Al-Mughrabi, who preaches at the Al-Aksa [sic] Mosque in Jerusalem, declared in his homily, "The Children of Israel ... would look for a small child, kidnap and steal him, bring a barrel called the barrel of nails ... They would put the small child in the barrel and his body would be pierced by these nails. In the bottom of the barrel, they would put a faucet and pour the blood" (2019, 220).

We cannot claim the blood libel is merely an aberration of history. It is a real and present issue which preachers and teachers, of Christian and of other faiths, have a duty to respond to. Teter's final words are an apt challenge to Christian leaders:

What the history of the blood libel also tells us is that political leadership matters, as do words and official statements. They might not always be effective nor prevent violence and hatred, but they provide a tangible trail of voices for those who want to turn into action and need moral support. For all the work behind the scenes to help Jews, the lack of an explicit public condemnation came to be read as a tacit approval. Silences are heard too (2020, 384).

This is a profound challenge. It is not enough to be silently horrified. We must act. Christian teachers and preachers have a duty to confront false teaching, in whatever form it takes. This would include repudiating and rejecting misleading and inaccurate portraits of first-century and contemporary Jews and Judaism. The blood libel is an extreme form of antisemitic prejudice that is unlikely to recur in a contemporary Christian setting. Nevertheless, I have heard Christians repeat the charge of deicide, or presume that all first-century Jews were racist legalists. These problems stem, at least in part, from inaccurate and unthought through teaching about Matthew's Gospel. The next chapter addresses this problem, making suggestions for how to preach from Matthew with Jewish people in mind.

Chapter 7
Preaching from Matthew with Jewish People in Mind

As noted above, Jewish scholar of the New Testament Amy-Jill Levine is clear that Christians are regularly guilty of stereotyping and sharing misinformation in their portrayal of first-century Judaism. Oversimplifying to the point of caricature, Levine's argument is that in a drive to make Jesus, and hence Christianity, unique, preachers tend to stereotype Judaism, making straw figures that can be easily knocked down with a rhetorical flourish proving the preacher's brilliance and affirming the congregation's choice to commit to Christ. Such behaviour is immoral and unworthy of a preacher of the Christian Good News.

This chapter offers suggestions to stimulate thought about how to preach from Matthew's Gospel with Jewish people in mind. Doubtless not every idea will be to the reader's taste; that is perfectly fine. This is not an exercise in enforcing an approach but rather an opportunity for critical reflection on the approach taken to preaching and teaching to date, and how it might change. There are five main sections. First, a discussion of the place of supersessionism and replacement theology. Second, an exploration of the views of scholars in the essay collection *Removing Anti-Judaism from the Pulpit*. Third, a discussion of a blog on "how to not be antisemitic." Fourth, an overview of Daniel Harrington's seven suggestions for how to approach Matthew. Fifth, Amy-Jill Levine's alphabet of suggestions for avoiding antisemitic actions or words.

Acknowledging supersessionism

In essence, supersessionism is the belief that Christians have replaced Jews as the covenant community of God. Another relevant term is "replacement theology," whereby "the followers of Jesus have replaced Israel 'according to the flesh' as those who are in right relationship with God" (Levine 2022,

1). There are at least two different forms of replacement theology: punitive and economic. The punitive view is that God punishes the Jews for their sins, including the sin of rejecting Jesus, by revoking the covenant and transferring its to the church. In the economic (functional) understanding, Christian rituals replace Jewish ones. Thus, baptism replaces circumcision, the Eucharist replaces the Temple sacrifices, the universal focus of the church replaces the ethnic specificity of the Jews and so forth.

It is relatively straightforward to find evidence of replacement theology within Matthew. In the First Gospel, Jesus is presented at the new Israel, who goes into and is then called out of Egypt, who "experiences as Exodus of sorts" at the River Jordan, who defeats the devil when tempted in the wilderness, who makes his disciples "the light of the world" (Matthew 5:14), who teaches as the new Moses, who in the parable of the Wicked Tenants tells of the death of the son and heir and tells his listeners "Therefore I tell you, the kingdom of God will be taken away from you and given to a people that produces the fruits of the kingdom" (Matthew 21:43), and who sends his followers out to make disciples of all nations (28:19). Levine concludes:

> For Matthew, whatever covenantal benefits accorded the Jews can be seen as having been transferred to the followers of Jesus, Jewish and gentile, but now seen as part of the *ekklesia*, the assembly gathered in Jesus's name, and not part of the *synagoga*, which, for Matthew, are alienated from the covenant community around Jesus (Levine 2022, 2).

Whilst there is plenty of evidence of replacement theology in other New Testament texts, this is sufficient for the present argument. It is clear that Matthew's Gospel can be read as advocating replacement theology. But the case is not explicit, and it is therefore incumbent upon the interpreter to do so responsibly. Levine also notes that all religious groups have a tendency towards supersessionism:

> All propose, albeit in various ways, that they have improved upon an anterior or rival tradition, and most argue that if they are right, then rival groups must be wrong or at least lacking (2022, 4).

At the very least, religious groups seek to persuade adherents of the truth and validity of their tradition. This might manifest as "soft supersessionism," which finds salvific value and a degree of superiority in the tradition in question, without denying the possibility of salvific value in other traditions. Conversely, "hard supersessionism" denies there is any soteriological worth in any other group. This is, of course, a matter of personal opinion and interpretation. But what seems incontrovertible is that the texts can be read in this way, and moreover, that the plain meaning of certain New Testament texts is, at the very least, in sympathy with replacement theology. It is, as Levine notes, more honest and useful for dialogue, to admit this fact rather than attempt to obfuscate or explain it away (Levine 2022, 5). This raises questions for the exegete and the preacher. There are ethical consequences to a supersessionist stance; the Nazis used superssionist rhetoric to justify their final solution to the "Jewish question." If Christians replace Jews in the covenant between God and his people, how then are Christians to treat Jewish people? And how are they to speak of them?

Removing anti-Judaism from the pulpit

It must be possible to be a faithful follower of Jesus without portraying Judaism or Jewish people inaccurately. The question is, how should this be done? The edited collection *Removing Anti-Judaism from the Pulpit* (Kee and Borowsky 1996) provides some possibilities. In the introduction, Borowsky notes the power of language, especially sacred language, presented in carefully curated books or powerful rhetoric from the pulpit. Borowsky recognises that whilst it was not the intention of the New Testament's authors to cause pain and suffering for Jewish people, nevertheless their words have been taken and used to justify this oppression. He argues that "words in Christian literature and liturgy taken out of context have been exploited by bigots in order to foster prejudice and distrust of the Jewish people" (1996, 7). A first point to note, therefore, is that preachers must be aware of the power of their words.

Marty recognises that most Christians listening to a sermon are not expecting an erudite academic exploration of the complexities of Christian anti-Judaism or antisemitism. Indeed, their faith is more likely to be focused on simple understanding of simple stories. But that does not mean complex issues should be ignored. Marty's main point is that one should not avoid the problematic and challenging texts, especially when faced with them in the lectionary. Rather one must read them, preach on them and help congregations wrestle with their own history (1996, 15-28). A second point to note, therefore, is that preachers and teachers should find appropriate contexts to help Christians wrestle with the difficult passages in their scriptures. Part of the problem is how little time Christians devote to studying their sacred texts and church history with academic and intellectual rigour. Developing a culture of serious study of the faith might help curb the possibility of antisemitism.

Williamson and Allen (1996, 36-42) identify four themes which they argue are prominent in anti-Jewish preaching. The first is the oversimplification that holds all Jews and Judaism as images of everything which is bad about religion. This may also manifest as being legalistic, committed to the past, with little or no interest in the spiritual dimension of religion. As Williamson and Allen note, this places Jewish people in a no-win situation: if they keep the law, they are legalists, if they ignore the law, they are hypocrites. The second theme builds on this, criticising Judaism and Jewish people, whilst leaving Christians with the impression that they are fine, with nothing to worry about. The third theme is that of replacement, proclaiming salvation as coming through Jesus alone. Williamson and Allen add that this can take universalist or inclusivist forms, contrasted with "the unfortunate particularism or exclusivism of the Jews" (1996, 40). Finally, the theme of conflict between Jesus and Jewish leaders dominates interpretation of the Gospels, so that scholars and preachers make this the only reading of the text.

Their suggestions for countering the tendency towards anti-Judaism are first, to recognise our freedom to interpret the text responsibly, especially if that text is polemical. Second, we must also recognise God's freedom to be gracious to whomsoever he chooses. Thus, we can recognise Jesus as a gift to humanity from God's unconditional love for Israel. But that does not mean God is not free to love those who do not accept Jesus. Divine love is for everyone. Third, preachers must recognise those texts which are not good news for everyone; in particular those texts that occur towards the end of Lent and in Holy Week that are bad news for Jews. They argue that preachers may need to preach "against the text" (1996, 42) if the situation demands it. This raises their third point, that texts must be contextualised, and preachers must beware of elevating themselves to a position of judgement, for it is God's role, not theirs, to judge. Whilst those of a more liberal theological position would be comfortable rejecting or revising sacred texts, those of a more conservative outlook face a harder task, of seeking to understand and explain texts that are heard as bad news by some.

Daly offers four homiletical strategies for removing anti-Judaism from the pulpit. The first is a sermon focused specifically on anti-Judaism, focusing in particular on why a supersessionist attitude is not acceptable theologically (understanding supersessionism as the belief that Christians have replaced Jews as the people of God; it entails a complete rejection of Jewish people as God's people). This type of sermon would require both an historical overview as well as basic theological education. Daly's second suggestion is to make anti-Judaism one central element of a sermon, if the chosen text(s) are amenable to such focus. Third, where the text is obviously open to anti-Jewish interpretation, this must be at least mentioned. Daly cites Mark 7:18, 14-15, 21-23, the lectionary Gospel for the twenty-second Sunday of the year in cycle B. This debate about internal versus external purity requires, Daly argues, comment on the nature of ancient polemical dialogue; the likelihood that Mark's community are projecting their own negative experiences of rejection onto the account; and the place of food laws within Jewish piety. Fourth, Daly argues all Christian sermons should have "a tone or attitude that interprets and proclaims every biblical text in a way that reveals its positive Jewish presuppositions and content" (1996, 57). It is in this fourth strategy that the most profound change will occur. The fourth main point is therefore a need for more learning, and for skilful deployment of that learning in everyday life and faith (1996, 50-57).

Holmgren discusses three misconceptions he believes many Christians have about Judaism. First, that Israelites and/or Jews are particularly rebellious, based on a misreading of the prophetic literature. Far from indicating a greater propensity to rebellion, Holmgren is clear that the literature indicates a greater sensitivity to individual and corporate sinfulness. The lesson of prophetic literature is, in fact, that all are in need of repentance. Second, that Jewish people do not believe the predictions of the Hebrew Bible. This misconception fails to recognise that there are no clear or unambiguous pointers towards Jesus of Nazareth as the fulfilment of the Jewish messianic hope. Rather the first followers of Jesus used passages from the Hebrew Scriptures to draw analogies and explain how they had come to conclude that Jesus was the Messiah. Third, the Hebrew Scriptures are regarded as antiquated, out-of-date and second rate. This means Christians fail to appreciate the riches of the Hebrew Scriptures, in particular the way they speak much more strongly to our daily experiences of the ups-and-downs of life than the New Testament texts do (1996, 67-74). The fifth main point is thus the importance of Christians learning more about historical and contemporary expressions of Judaism, including getting to know Jewish people for themselves, a not entirely simple task given the difference in numbers of Christians and Jews in the UK today, not to mention the fact that many Jewish people live in north London and specific areas of Manchester.

Not every preacher will agree with every suggestion here, and it is certainly not my purpose to dictate how sermons should be preached. But recognising that there is an issue which requires careful consideration is a useful place to begin. Christians, especially those of an exclusivist persuasion, who believe all must explicitly profess faith in Christ in order to enter into a saving relationship with God, would do well to recognise that whilst they think they are sharing good news, not everyone hears it that way. Equally, those who attempt a revisionist approach whereby all references to "Jews" in the New Testament are altered to "Judeans" risk erasing Judaism from Christian scripture, which would in and of itself be a form of Christian anti-Judaism. There are no easy answers, but solutions must be sought.

An evangelical Christian argument about "how to not be antisemitic"

On Sunday 8th May 2022, the Anglican Diocese of Oxford held a service to mark the 800th anniversary (one day early) of the Synod of Oxford of 9th May 1222 which introduced the first measures against Jews in England, and led to more harsh measures and the eventual expulsion of Jews from England in 1290. Writing in response to discussion about apologies and repentance by Christians in relation to this shameful history, the evangelical blogger Ian Paul suggested twelve views, which many Christians hold, that perpetuate anti-Judaism, and could lead to antisemitism. What follows is a near verbatim extract from that blog (https://www.psephizo.com/biblical-studies/how-not-to-be-antisemitic/):

1. Jesus rejected the law

It is quite common to hear people comment that Jesus rejected the law and its legalism, and modelled a kind of free-wheeling gospel of grace where the law does not matter. Ian Paul proposes this thinking is based on a simplistic reading of the "you have heard it said, but I say to you…" language in the Sermon on the Mount in Matthew 5 to 7, from seeing the criticisms by the Pharisees of Jesus' apparent lax approach to practices they insisted on (such as Sabbath observance and ritual washing), and from Jesus' association with "sinners." But this is an inaccurate reading; Jesus was a Torah-observant Jew, who called his followers to a stricter, not laxer, observance of the law, in demanding that outward observance on its own was not enough.

2. Jesus saves us from "religion"

It is argued that Jesus was not "religious," but hung around with "non-religious" people on the margins, and his main criticisms were reserved for the religious. But if this reconstruction is true, it is quite hard not to read this as seriously antisemitic, since the only religious people around in the gospels were Jewish people. But this claim includes at least three mistaken assumptions.

First, the world of the first century was a religious world quite distinct from our contemporary Western culture where we have compartmentalised "religion" into a neat, distinct, category. Essentially, in the ancient world everyone was religious, even those "on the margins." Secondly, the good news is directed towards and appeals to both the observant and the lax, the pious and the marginal. Luke's gospel is particularly explicit here: almost all of the main players in the narrative are pious, observant, devout Jews, and it is to these whom God reveals himself first. Thirdly, Jesus spent time with the outcasts in order to call them to pious holiness, not to leave them as they were.

3. The Pharisees were all bad

The sharpest conflicts in the gospels often appear to be between Jesus and the Pharisees, who were a primarily lay-led purity movement, and who were ambivalent about the power plays of those who were associated with the temple. They are often depicted as amongst those challenging and questioning Jesus, and join in the conspiracy to do away with him, and Jesus appears to reserve his harshest words for them. Yet Pharisees were also drawn to the ministry of John the Baptist to be baptised (Matthew 3:7); many of them come and attend to Jesus' teaching and want to defend him (Luke 7:35; 13:31). Moreover, Jesus urges his disciples to attend to the teaching of the Pharisees (Matthew 23:2-3).

4. The love of God is unconditional and works don't count

Whilst many argue God accepts us as we are, regardless of what we've done, Ian Paul suggests the message of the New Testament is "God loves you and therefore calls you to change; at great cost he deals with your sin, what is wrong in the world, in order that you might live a changed life." The apparent contrast between the language of faith and works in James 2:18-24 and Romans 3–4 is just that: apparent. The debate here is precisely around the grounds on which we are saved (grace) and what we are saved for (good works), so that saving faith makes itself seen in a changed life. This is vital to avoid the caricature of "works-based Judaism" contrasted with "grace-filled Christianity."

5. Grace has replaced law

One of the most striking and repeated refrains in the Old Testament is "The Lord is gracious and compassionate, slow to anger and rich in love" (Exodus 34:6; Numbers 14:18; Psalms 86:15; 103:8; 145:8). So how is it that many people come to read the Scriptures as being about a demanding, law-giving (Jewish) God who is constantly angry, and a loving, meek (Christian) Jesus who loves us and accepts us just as we are? There is no doubt that Jesus came close to those who were far away, and touched them with the healing compassion of God, just as there is no doubt that Jesus talked more about the need for radical change and the danger of eternal destruction than anyone else in the New Testament. The grace of God in Jesus is an even greater outpouring of the grace God had already bestowed on his people Israel, not a contrast to it. God rescued his people first, and only then gave them the Commandments to shape their new life together in response to his saving acts.

6. "The Jews" were opposed to Jesus

In the Fourth Gospel, there are moments where it appears that "the Jews" are the ones who oppose Jesus, and taken out of context (as this language has often, tragically, been) it could be read as contrasting Jewish opponents of Jesus with his "Christian" followers. This is, of course, both historical and narrative nonsense. All the characters in the Fourth Gospel are Jews, including Jesus and his followers, so we need to read this language more carefully (see Wilson 2020, 51-78).

7. Paul thought the law was bad

Protestant reading of Paul has been deeply shaped by the Reformation, and a general outlook of the contrast in Paul between "works righteousness" versus "salvation by grace." This is why it is important to consider the (now not very new) "new perspective" on Paul which offers a more historically rooted reading of Paul and of first-century Judaism(s), and takes seriously the positive as well as negative things Paul says about the law (see for example Wright 2013a, 2013b).

8. The Church is contrasted with Israel

There is a good case for never using the word "church" in English translations, for two reasons. First, we cannot read that word without including with it associations of either institutions ("the Church of England") or buildings ("St Botolph's Church") neither of which belong in the New Testament. But, second, we miss a vital point of continuity: the word *ekklesia* was used of the gathering of citizens (that is, free men over the age of 30) for decision-making within the Greek *polis*, but it was also the word used in the Greek translation of the Old Testament for the "congregation of the sons of Israel," that is, the people of God.

We should therefore read the word "church" as having continuity with, not differentiation from, Israel. Paul is very clear that gentile believers are grafted into the Israel of God, neither replacing it as "the Church" nor being absorbed into it by becoming Jews. And John is clear, in Revelation 7, that the ordered, holy Israel of God (the 144,000 that he hears counted out) is now drawn from every tribe, language, people and nation. In the Christian understanding, the Israel of God is still Israel, but it now includes both ethnic Jews and gentiles from every ethnicity, nation, culture, and language.

9. Jesus is not the Jewish Messiah

Evangelism amongst Jewish people is a uniquely sensitive issue, in part because of the history of forced conversion and abuse visited upon Jews in European Christendom. But there is a strange paradox in the idea that a movement, which was entirely a Jewish renewal movement in its earliest days, following a Jewish messiah, and made up entirely of Jewish followers, should not now ever include Jews amongst its numbers. For a nuanced discussion of this question from an Anglican Christian perspective, see *God's Unfailing Word* (Archbishops' Council 2019). There are strongly held views within this debate; some Jewish people who have become followers of Jesus argue strongly for the freedom to evangelise. Other Jewish people find the very notion of evangelism amongst Jewish people offensive, as the Chief Rabbi, Ephraim Mirvis, makes clear in the afterword to *God's Unfailing Word*.

10. Modern Israel is a uniquely evil oppressor

There are many who believe that the existence of the modern state of Israel is a sign of God's faithfulness and, in particular, fulfilment of his "end times" plan. But Ian Paul rejects this view. One of the many problems with this view is that modern Israel is treated with ethnical exceptionalism, and that to question anything that happens there is to challenge God's plans. On the other hand, many others think that Israel is an almost unique oppressor of Palestinian Arabs, claiming that Israel is an apartheid state. Neither of these perspectives is especially helpful in developing nuanced debate. Discussion of this issue is completely outside the scope of this book, but resources such as CCJ 2020 are a helpful place to start.

11. The suffering of the Jews is mere history

Ian Paul recounts that on one of his trips to Israel, he was in a group which had the chance to meet political and religious leaders from all sides of the current political dispute. That included meeting with members of the PLO's negotiating team who had been working with Israeli leaders in the conversations about future peace. He asked one of them: "How important do you think the Holocaust is for those you have been negotiating with?" His reply was shocking: "Well, it was unfortunate." He appeared to have no understanding of how central the Holocaust is in the thinking of those with whom he was negotiating.

We need to understand how important the painful history of antisemitism is for Jewish people, and confront its reality (see, for example Grunwald-Spier 2016, Rittner et al 2000).

12. Jesus is a non-Jewish everyman

Jesus relates to all people everywhere, and so has universal significance. But he does so from the particularity of the incarnation, as a first-century Jewish man. All attempts to erase this identity include within them the seeds of anti-Jewish thinking. The best antidote to this approach is taking seriously what the gospels say about Jesus the Jewish messiah, whose grace has flowed from this place into all the world. Salvation is of the Jews. Ian Paul concludes:

> In my own journey of discipleship and scholarship, I have been immensely helped by engaging with Jewish scholars and thinkers, reading Jewish commentaries on the Old Testament, and listening to orthodox Jewish critiques of contemporary culture. These are things every Christian leader—every Christian—ought to be engaged with.

Responding to Ian Paul's suggestions

This is a helpful list for Christian preachers and teachers. The wide-ranging nature of the blog means that much of what is discussed has fallen outside of the scope of this book; hence references are included for those who want to delve in to any topic in greater detail. At the heart Ian Paul's suggestions is a call to more serious scholarship; for preachers and teachers to be diligent in their preparation, to read widely and to consider the implications of what they say and write. There is, of course, space for a wide variety of views on the controversial topics referenced above, and it is not my intention to dictate how people think. Rather the point is to provide further opportunities for reflection on how we can be true to our convictions whilst also bearing Jewish people in mind (on which see Bayfield 2017, LeDonne and Behrendt 2017, Wilson 2019).

Daniel J. Harrington on problems and opportunities in Matthew

Turning from general observations to the specific issue of how to preach and teach from Matthew's Gospel, Daniel Harrington outlines seven potential problems that he argues should in fact be seen as opportunities for Christian teachers and preachers to "address positively and constructively issues that are at the heart of Christian life" (2007, 417). First, that Matthew's Christology has many unique points, not least the birth narratives and genealogy, never mind the resurrection appearances. The five discourses: the Sermon on the Mount (Matthew 5-7); teaching on Mission (Matthew 10); the parables (Matthew 13); the discussion of community life (Matthew 18) and of eschatology (Matthew 24-25) bring a uniquely Jewish flavour to Matthew's portrayal of Jesus, as does his use of Christological titles.

Second, the Sermon on the Mount, which must be read in the context of Jesus' mission. Harrington reads it as part of the story of Jesus, setting out how Jesus believes people can live in right relationship with God and their fellow human beings. It should be understood as standing in a long line of Jewish wisdom teaching.

Third, Harrington tackles potential anti-Judaism. He states: "Christian teachers and preachers must admit at least the anti-Jewish potential of certain elements of Matthew's Gospel" (2007, 420), but also questions whether Matthew himself was anti-Jewish. Harrington proposes that the Matthean community was likely to have been largely Jewish, and that the harsh language in the text is part of an intra-Jewish debate precipitated by the destruction of the Jerusalem temple in 70 CE. There is therefore an opportunity for Christian teachers and preachers to help their congregations to understand the nuances and complexity of this debate, introducing the various key characters. Equally, the so-called fulfilment quotations should spur a renewed enthusiasm and detailed study of the Hebrew scriptures. Thus "the problem of Matthew's alleged anti-Judaism can be turned into an opportunity for better appreciating first-century Judaism and Matthew's place in it" (2007, 420).

Fourth, Matthew's patriarchalism; Harrington admits that women have a less prominent role than in other Gospels, but nevertheless finds moments of significant conversation and some key characters, such as the Canaanite woman in 15:21-28, particularly because Jesus seems to lose the argument.

Fifth, Matthew is very positive about the Mosaic law. Harrington argues that the Matthean community was "a Jewish form of Christianity and regarded themselves as still a sect within Judaism," even if other Jews disagreed with that assessment. Harrington proposes that Matthean Christianity was in tension with Pauline Christianity, and that the latter was ultimately more successful. He goes so far as to suggest Matthew's Christianity "represents to some extent a road not taken or even a dead end" (2007, 421). This, Harrington concludes, teaches us to recognise and value theological diversity. Harrington also finds a tension within Matthew; a tension between the expectation of obedience to the Mosaic Law and Jesus' own status as Emmanuel, God with us, which "transcends the letter of the Mosaic law" (2007, 422).

Sixth, Matthew's eschatology is challenging to interpret, but Harrington suggests it provides a framework for the Christian life. He sees it offering a balanced focus on both the present and the future, seen in the Lord's prayer (6:9-13), the parables of the kingdom (13) and the eschatological discourse (24-25). Disciples of Jesus in whatever age must live as aspirational citizens of the kingdom of heaven.

Seventh, Jesus' final cry of dereliction, which in Matthew particularly, expands on Psalm 22 and Isaiah 53. Harrington rejects what he terms "romantic and existentialist speculations about final despair of Jesus' part" (2007, 423), arguing instead that interpretation should focus on the Hebrew scriptures. Psalm 22 is an individual lament, in which the complainant addresses personal despair to God, but also expresses confidence in God based both on personal experience and Israel's history. The Psalmist also looks forward to future vindication and celebration with God. The whole Psalm must be read when considering Jesus' cry of despair.

Although Harrington singles out addressing anti-Judaism as one particular problem amongst the seven issues he tackles, it does also link with the other six he discusses. Christology, eschatology, the teaching of the Sermon on the Mount, attitude to the Mosaic law, the problem of patriarchy and Jesus' death can all be exposited in an anti-Jewish way. The challenge for the preacher is to plan a more sophisticated response that locates text in context, recognises the history of interpretation, and provides a confident, but not arrogant or abusive message for the listening congregation. We can recognise the Jewish origins of Matthew's Gospel, but we must also acknowledge that the text can easily be interpreted through a framework of replacement theology. How do we do that whilst remaining good neighbours to our Jewish friends and colleagues? What place do we give to Matthean theology, especially if we agree with Harrington's idea that it is very positive about Torah observance? How do we hold tightly to belief in Jesus as Messiah, but simultaneously hold that belief lightly enough to remain in positive relationship with those who disagree with us? These are the types of questions that preachers and teachers need to wrestle with as they read and interpret Matthew's Gospel.

An alphabet of suggestions

In her book *The Misunderstood Jew*, Amy-Jill Levine offers an "alphabet of suggestions" of how Christians and Jews can build more positive relationships (2006, 215-26).

First, avoid generalisation. That is, don't say "all Jews think…" or "all Jews are …" This is equally true for Christianity. Neither faith is monolithic now, or was it in the first-century. There is diversity both within and between denominations, and the best way to understand this is to attend worship with a variety of Christians and Jews.

Second, recognise that Jewish and Christian texts "contain ugly, misogynistic, intolerant and hateful material" (2006, 216). We must acknowledge both the good and the bad if dialogue is to be meaningful.

Third, avoid selective citation, whether of the Church Fathers or of rabbinic sources. Levine notes that scholars often short-cut, simply citing a text from another scholar's work, without checking the source for themselves. This dangerous, and lazy, tendency, can easily lead to misrepresentation, where a quote is taken out of context.

Fourth, don't divorce Jesus from the Jewish people. Jesus did not speak against Jews or Judaism, but he spoke *to* Jews from *within* Judaism. But at the same time, Jesus must be understood as provocative; after all some of those who heard him left home and family to follow him, whilst others decided he was demon-possessed or insane. Levine urges Christians to recognise Jesus in his Jewish context, but to resist the urge to appropriate Jewish practices as their own.

Fifth, study of biblical material necessarily includes study of interpretation. Whilst Paul's letter to the Galatians concerns the debate as to whether male followers of Jesus must be circumcised, this is not an issue for Christians today. In the same way, a literalist reading Ezekiel or Leviticus will not tell you what Jewish people are focused on.

Sixth, both history generally, and religious competition particularly, are very messy. The Gospels are subjective accounts of the views of those within a religious conflict. The first Christians were, Levine explains, a struggling minority, and like most sectarian groups under pressure, they defined themselves over against the majority whom they opposed. As time passed, and Christianity became predominantly gentile, Jewish followers of Jesus found themselves in the minority, and were eventually classed as heretics. "In deciding who it was, the church defined itself over and against the synagogue, and the synagogue reciprocated" (2006, 218). Most Jews simply did not recognise Jesus as inaugurating the messianic age, but from a Christian perspective, this was interpreted as stubborn refusal to recognise the work of God and/or being misled by blind leaders who were even called children of the devil by John.

Seventh, be aware that the same word can have a completely different meaning in a different context. Levine cites examples such as what is meant by "Bible" or "messiah," as well as differences in custom or practice. Whilst many Christians might take money to church to give as an offering to God, Jewish people would never do this, for the Sabbath is a day of rest, not of trade.

Eighth, beware of artificial connection and don't be afraid to disagree. Levine argues that "Judaeo-Christian" is a politically expedient term which really means the Old Testament, as interpreted by Christians, together with the Christian faith. After the first few centuries CE, Christians were no more Jewish than Jews were Christian.

Ninth, beware of Marcionism. Marcion was a mid-second century Christian who distinguished between the (Jewish) God of the Old Testament and the (Christian) God of the New. The most common modern form of this heresy is the notion of an Old Testament God of wrath and a New Testament God of love.

Tenth, Christians and Jews ought to know their own history before engaging in interfaith work. This is particularly true for Christian leaders, both to facilitate their teaching ministry and also to ensure they are appropriately sensitive when engaging in interfaith conversations.

Eleventh, Levine encourages the reading of scripture in an interfaith setting. This is to enable us to hear with "other ears," recognising the impact a text might have on someone who sees the world very differently. Utilising the example of a short-hand reference to a desire for a day when there is "no longer Jew or Greek," Levine notes the desire in citing Galatians 3:26 is promotion of unity, but explains it might be heard by a Jewish person as a wish to eradicate all Jews.

Twelfth, speak out where necessary. Levine recounts personal experience of approaching authors whose material she deemed antisemitic or anti-Jewish, explaining it is not necessarily an especially productive approach, as the author in question may simply ignore the suggestions made. There is, therefore, a need to raise public awareness of the problem, not to condemn individuals, but to ensure people are aware of the issues at stake.

Thirteenth, hymns can also be antisemitic, as can devotional literature. This may not be what the author intended, but it might be how the text is heard.

Fourteenth, be aware that the lectionary might convey anti-Jewish impressions. Levine argues that preachers "need to be alert for the slippage that sometimes occurs between what the texts say and the impression that can be conveyed to the congregation" (2006, 222). What you say matters less than how you are heard.

Fifteenth, be clear as to why Jesus was crucified. It was not, Levine argues, because of his teaching that the poor were closer to the kingdom of heaven than the rich, or because he rejected the Torah or taught love of God and neighbour. Jesus was executed because he was proclaimed king in Roman-occupied Jerusalem and was thus a political liability.

Sixteenth, Levine instructs us to "park guilt and entitlement at the door before engaging in interfaith conversation" (2006, 222). She warns Christians against feeling so guilty about Christian antisemitism that they do not share their faith in Jesus as divine messiah and Son of God. Equally, Jewish people can come seeking apologies not engagement. But since Christians today are not responsible for the past and Jews today cannot grant forgiveness for past failures, neither approach is helpful.

Seventeenth, be aware of how you pray in public. Levine does not like what she terms "parochial" prayer, such as prayer in Jesus' name, but nor does she approve of watered-down anaemic prayers. She wants both Jews and Christians to find a *via media*.

Eighteenth, do not bear false witness against your neighbour. That is, represent the historical facts fairly and maintain intellectual rigour in your arguments.

Nineteenth, Christians must think carefully about how evangelistic outreach is heard and experienced. Levine is clear that Jews need to hear the sincerity of Christians' message, that it is offered out of love and concern. Equally Christians need to respect the integrity of the Jewish position which denies the truth of the Christian claim. She adds that if Jews are concerned about Christians trying to convert their children, the best thing is to teach them Judaism in an authentic and engaging way. For Christians, Levine suggests they step up and engage in social justice concerns, and only when they are asked why should they explain their faith.

Twentieth, be especially careful when talking about the Middle East; there are many perspectives on the history and possible solutions.

Twenty-first, check that those responsible for educating children are themselves informed about the history of their own tradition, as well as the history of the other. It is all too easy for well-meaning but ill-informed teachers to share bigotry and prejudice.

Twenty-second, learn Hebrew and Greek if possible, and read other first-century texts such as the Dead Sea Scrolls, the Apocrypha, Josephus, Philo and so forth. We do not live in the first-century, and it is very easy to impose our own understanding and values on the texts we read.

Twenty-third, be careful when using the internet. Antisemitic groups have established pages that selectively cite texts to portray Judaism negatively. Check the veracity of the source material and the perspective of the site's author.

Twenty-fourth, Levine recommends we practise holy envy, looking at the other tradition with generosity and seeking to see the good in what we find there.

Twenty-fifth, Levine recommends that as a last resort, use psychological manipulation. She explains:

> At Vanderbilt, I have been known to bring my son to my class. I introduce him to my students and then I say: "When you speak of Jews, picture this kid in the front pew. Don't say anything that will hurt this child, and don't say anything that will cause a member of your congregation to hurt this child." I grant that the move is

theatrical and manipulative; it's also remarkably effective (2006, 226).

Twenty-sixth, Levine concludes that she also asks her students to imagine she is standing at the back of a church when they are preaching and that she will object if they say something that is inappropriate or offensive.

Doubtless readers will object to some of Levine's proposals; my purpose in reproducing them is not to insist they are all followed to the letter, but rather to note the need for an attitudinal and tonal shift in much Christian teaching and preaching. Misrepresentation, stereotyping, lazy condemnation and hypocrisy have no place in the church, least of all in the pulpit.

What practical steps can preachers take?

In an edited collection on the Pharisees, Amy-Jill Levine discusses how portraying Pharisees specifically, and Jews generally, as evil, results in antisemitism. She offers possible solutions to the problem. She recognises that most who teach the New Testament today do not want to share anything antisemitic, but nevertheless they do so. This is primarily because they are culturally deaf to the impact of their words, and lack the time to address their congregations' implicit biases in homilies of only a few minutes. Furthermore, there is the issue of common parlance, where Pharisee is a synonym for hypocrite. Levine also identifies failures in the academy; seminaries in particular do not address the problems properly. Finally, prejudice and misinformation about Pharisees is regularly taught in Sunday schools the world over. Levine offers solutions: labelling discriminatory art, providing historical information in the church bulletin, utilising resources specifically written to help the preacher avoid antisemitism, as well as teaching more generally on the history of Christian-Jewish relations. Perhaps most importantly, Levine encourages Christians to work with Jewish people in developing appropriate responses. This is arguably the most important step; seek out Jewish people to support you in learning how to preach from Matthew's Gospel with Jewish people in mind (2021, 403-27).

Conclusions

The purpose of this chapter is to encourage Christians, especially those with a teaching and preaching ministry, to reflect critically and honestly on their practice. I have deliberately included a broad range of perspectives and understandings; not all of what is written here will be agreeable to everyone, but there is plenty of food for thought. But it must not remain as only thought; it should transform and change practice as well. It is perhaps particularly profitable to consider those suggestions that the reader finds most objectionable. What is it about them that is problematic? Is it poor reasoning? An unfounded argument? Or a truth that is too painful to acknowledge? There are too many suggestions here for everything to be enacted. But there are plenty to ensure at least one or two are utilised to enable preaching and teaching with Jewish people in mind.

Chapter 8
Sample Sermons

This chapter contains some short sample sermons. They are not written to present definitive solutions to the problem of how to preach from Matthew's Gospel in a way that recognises the antisemitic potential of the text but also is faithful to the Christian good news. Rather they are first attempts, deliberately short, recognising that many congregations expect a sermon of only ten to twelve minutes. I am sure you and other preachers can do a far better job than I have here. But hopefully this presents, at the very least, a place to begin.

Sample sermon on Matthew 5:17-20

It won't hurt anyone if I do it. Speed limits are stupid. It's perfectly safe to drive at 40 mph here. There's no one about. No traffic. No people. And I'm late anyway.

There's a narrative around rule breaking that normally begins with self-justification. Most of us don't intentionally break the law of the land, but if we are honest, we have to admit to failing to fulfil all the commands of God. I don't think things were any different in Jesus' day. As we spend a few minutes considering Jesus' words in Matthew 5, we would do well to remember that people always have wanted, and always will want, to run their own lives. Yet the Christian tradition teaches us that our own attempts inevitably end in hurt and failure, for ourselves as much as for those around us. That is why Jesus teaches in Matthew 5 about the importance of obeying the law of God.

Scholars of the New Testament like to debate the purpose of the Sermon on the Mount. Does Matthew record it to show us the expected standard of behaviour in the kingdom of the heavens, a list of rules for how to live as one of God's children? Or is it setting out how impossible it is to live God's way? A kind of "impossible ethic" that's designed to make you realise how awful you are and drive you to faith in Christ? Or maybe both at once, a standard to strive towards even if you know you'll never quite make it?

It's fair to say that in Jesus' day there was an awful lot of debate about how to follow God, how to live faithfully according to the Torah, the Law of God. And Jesus puts himself right in the centre of that debate. Various bits of the Sermon on the Mount position Jesus in different debates of his day. This isn't the time or the place to go into the detail, but it is worth reading around the subject, finding out what other people in the first-century thought and taught, just so you can understand Jesus' teaching a bit better.

If we think about our passage, Matthew 5:17-20, it's clear that some people thought Jesus was saying the Torah is irrelevant. We have to remember that although they appear first in our New Testament, the Gospels were almost certainly written down after many of Paul's letters were sent. And Paul clearly did teach that gentile followers of Jesus, that is, those followers of Jesus who were not Jewish, did not have to obey the Torah, the Jewish law, in full. You may recall in some of his letters Paul gets quite cross, insisting men don't need to be circumcised to become followers of Jesus. Maybe Paul's teaching was in the air when Matthew wrote, and so he sets out how he understands the situation of those early gentile followers of Jesus. If you read through Matthew's Gospel, you'll find a conspicuous absence of mention of circumcision, so presumably Matthew agreed on that point at least.

But for Matthew, obeying the Torah seems important. Which brings us to the crucial question. What exactly does Jesus mean in these verses? It strikes me that if we recognise that in this conversation Jesus is addressing Jewish people, then it's fairly clear he's telling them to keep on doing what they've always done. That is to say, for a first-century Jewish person, who is interested in following Jesus, who thinks he might be the Messiah, there was a continuing obligation to obey the commands of the Torah. I may be a new teacher, Jesus is saying, but I'm not letting go of the teaching our people have received down the centuries.

This much is clear in the passages that follow. Jesus doesn't negate the commands of the Torah, but rather intensifies them, going right to the heart of the matter. It's not just the physical act of murder that's a problem. Hatred or contempt which might lead to murder are a problem. It's not just the act of adultery that's a problem. All forms of sexual lust are bad. And so on.

That much is fair enough. But what about fulfilment? What does it mean that Jesus fulfils the Torah of God? Jesus appears to expect his Jewish audience to obey all the commands of the Torah. At the same time, he also says he has come to fulfil the commands, which must mean something more than just that Jesus obeys the commands as well. Matthew makes a lot of how he finds fulfilment of the Hebrew scriptures in the person and life, death and resurrection of Jesus. It's as if he sees a divine plan that God is working out through Jesus, to bring all things to their intended goal, of restored relationship and creation renewed.

In Jesus, that process of renewal and restoration begins, and we are invited to play our part, by living kingdom focused lives, striving to glorify God in our attitudes and actions, which recognise that hatred is equal to murder, or lust is as damaging as adultery. We try and shape everything we do and say according to the standards and ethics of God's kingdom.

The first Christians argued amongst themselves as to whether new followers of Jesus had to obey all the Torah in order to be disciples of Jesus. The conclusion was yes to the ethics, but no to other laws, which is why Christians today are not bound by restrictions in what we eat or what we wear for example. Whether Matthew would've agreed is a moot point. Part of me wonders if he'd look at how many Christians live today, and be shocked at how casual an attitude we have to worship and our relationship with God. I'm sure he would be outraged, saddened and disbelieving of any who tried to take this section of his gospel and create a lie that Judaism is legalistic where Christianity is free.

For that is not at all what Jesus is teaching. Granted the now almost entirely gentile church has concluded we are no longer bound by all the stipulations of the Torah. But we are bound by the ethical standards of God, which expect us to speak nothing but love and mercy, care and compassion for those individuals with whom we disagree. And we owe the Jewish people a great debt of gratitude for their preservation of the Hebrew scriptures, not to mention recognising how badly Christians have treated Jewish people down the centuries.

As followers of Jesus, we are called to be righteous and holy, striving to be the very best we can be, which was, after all precisely what the scribes and Pharisees were doing, giving their all to be holy and Godly people in a perverse and perverted world. In Jesus we are set a perfect standard, one which we will inevitably all fall short of. But that need not trouble us, for the Lord tells us that his power is made perfect in our weakness, and it is when we are weak that he is strong.

Gracious God, we admit our weakness and failures, especially our inability to love you with all our heart, soul, mind and strength. We confess also our sin in judging others. Help us to trust all things into your hands as we seek to serve you. Amen.

Sample sermon on Matthew 16

I can still remember the moment, and it makes me smile every time I think about it. I was doing a fairly bread-and-butter piece of work, facilitating an encounter between some Christian young people, who were taking a gap year to work for local churches, and a Buddhist monk. It was part of the interns' training, to meet with people of other faiths, to learn how to dialogue with them. Being young and idealistic evangelicals, the interns were keen to try and convert the people they met. One young lady tried a very direct approach, "So what do you think about Jesus?" she asked, earnestly.

The monk paused and considered the question carefully. After a significant silence, he replied, "I don't."

"Sorry?"

"I don't think about Jesus at all."

What's your normal reaction to people you disagree with? How do you cope when your view of the world isn't shared by the person you're talking with? For some of us, that can be a highly energising experience, a chance to test the validity of our own assumptions, maybe give one or two of our sacred cows a push, and see if they stand solid, or if they fall over. But for other people, encountering those who see the world differently is a remarkably unsettling experience.

Thinking back over the encounter between the Christian and the Buddhist, it was clear that this was a difficult experience for her. She presumed everyone was interested in talking about Jesus. But many people aren't. That's the question I would like to spend a few minutes thinking about, posing the question slightly more sharply. How do we relate to those who say no? What's our response to people who have no interest at all in Jesus of Nazareth? It's fairly obvious the UK is full of them, as our churches aren't full by any means. What are your options?

Matthew 16 might give us some ideas. In verse thirteen, Jesus asks what the word on the street is about him, and his disciples reply in verse fourteen, outlining Elijah, John the Baptist, Jeremiah, one of the prophets as options. This can be very roughly translated as meaning most people think Jesus is some sort of a messenger from God, possibly even the herald of the Messiah, for that was a role assigned to Elijah. "Prophet" presumably also means "a good thing but also potentially a trouble maker, someone who might be confrontational, stir things up." It's not necessarily a complement.

Then Peter says what he thinks, that Jesus is the Messiah, before proceeding to show that he doesn't really understand what that means, because he gets all twitchy at the possibility of Jesus dying on a cross to atone for the sins of the whole world.

It's easy to be rude about Peter, but that's unfair because "Messiah who dies for the sins of everyone" wasn't a category that was immediately obvious to first century Jews, any more than it is immediately obvious to most people today. For the Christian, through the eyes of faith, opened and equipped by the Holy Spirit, it may be obvious. But that ain't necessarily so for everyone else.

Indeed, for many Jewish people, what they hear here is nothing short of blasphemy. And that's at least part of the reason why Jesus is condemned to death at the instigation of the Jewish religious authorities. He was a political pain and a religious rule breaker, because his claims were heard as blasphemy, a capital crime.

At the heart of this chapter, indeed at the heart of Matthew's Gospel, is an argument between first century Jewish people about whether Jesus of Nazareth is the Son of God, the one come to redeem the world. Some Jewish people decided yes, and became his followers. Then eventually, after all sorts of stuff happening, we ended up with Christianity today, where hardly any of Jesus' current followers have any real Jewish heritage. And that presents us with a challenge. How do we relate to the descendants of those who decided, for whatever reason, to reject Jesus and follow a different path?

Christians have caused untold harm to Jewish people down the centuries, and we should be mindful of that reality in any encounters we have today.

For me, at least, the following two principles apply. First, respect the right of other people to make their own choices. Far too much of Christian history is littered with the fall-out of compulsion. You can't force people to follow Jesus, and any attempts at coercion are unethical and counter-productive.

Second, live in such a way that any presentation of the Christian Gospel, whether that's in words or actions or both, are clearly heard as an attempt at sharing good news. People might not believe it's good news for them personally, but if they experience you as a person of integrity and honesty, justice and truth, then even if they disagree with you, they're not going to be harmed by what you say or do. In Matthew 16, Jesus is clear that the road of a disciple is one of appropriate self-denial, of surrender to Christ and of a fullness of life found only in and through relationship with him.

It's easy to be flummoxed by a Buddhist monk who says he never thinks about Jesus. And why would he, if he never encounters Christians who radiate Jesus in all they think and do and speak? There's a promise in this passage that the church will prevail, and I'm sure it will. But I think there's a warning in those words as well, that if we aren't living the lives of those who have taken up our crosses and followed Jesus, then what evidence will there be that the church is flourishing in our land?

There are all sorts of complicated, and dispiriting, bits of history, that we have to contend with. There are some very specific questions about how Christians relate to Jewish people, how we portray first century Jews in our sermons and what connections we draw with the present day. There are more general questions about how we relate to people of other faith and belief perspectives, what is ethical, what is right, what we can do, what we should avoid. It's easy to feel overwhelmed.

But ultimately, it comes back to one thing, the command to love, to seek for others what you would have them seek for yourself. To die to self, to personal ambition and one's own agenda, preferring the good of all over selfish gain. If we seek to live up to this standard, then the gates of hell will not prevail against us.

Lord God, help us to live with such devotion to Christ that his light is a compelling beacon in our lives. Forgive us where our witness has been poor or indifferent. May our lives, our words, our actions, speak to all we meet of Christ's glory, to the praise of your name. Amen.

Sample sermon on Matthew 23

You have probably come across the chart that has done the rounds on social media that contrasts what the English say, what the English mean, and what other people hear. I'll remind you of a few of them.

Take the English phrase "I hear what you say." That means "I disagree and do not want to discuss it any further," but what is heard is "He accepts my point of view."

Or take "With the greatest respect," that is to say, "I think you're an idiot," which the non-native speaker hears as "She respects me."

"Oh, incidentally," which is heard as "this is not very important," when it actually means "this is the main point I want to make."

I could go on, but the point is, I hope, clear. Different cultures use different styles of language in different contexts. If you leave aside Speaker's Corner and Prime Minister's Questions in the House of Commons, the UK generally, and the English particularly, especially the English in the South East, really don't do polemical debate at all.

Which means reading Matthew 23 is culturally challenging for us. In some parts of the world, this is how people still debate today, but for us in the UK it might just sound rude and unacceptable. When we read polemical texts like this one it's helpful to bear in mind that the main purpose of polemic is to persuade, and often to persuade someone that they made the right choice in joining our group, and those other people are terrible, and you really shouldn't have anything to do with them.

Notice how chapter 23 begins. Jesus is talking to the crowds and his disciples, not to the Pharisees. That is to say, this is what you might call "internally focused polemic," aimed at encouraging the disciples in particular, as well as anyone listening in the crowd who is sympathetic, that Jesus is right and the Pharisees are wrong. He is modelling a particular approach to leadership, establishing his credentials, in part by doing down his opponents, using the conventional style of the day.

Let me give you an example, from *The Testament of Levi*, part of the *Testaments of the Twelve Patriarchs*, a text probably written by a Greek speaking Jew who lived a couple of hundred years before Jesus. The section I'm quoting from speaks judgement on religious hypocrisy:

> You shall set aside the Law and nullify the words of the prophets by your wicked perversity. You persecute just men: and you hate the pious; the word of the faithful you regard with revulsion. A man who by the power of the Most High renews the Law you name

'Deceiver,' and finally you shall plot to kill him, not discerning his eminence; by your wickedness you take innocent blood on your heads (*Testament of Levi* 16:2-4).

There's plenty more of it in the literature of the day, but that's enough for now. The first thing to note, then, is that plenty of people were polemical in the first century. But does that mean we can be comfortable with Jesus being polemical?

I think there are two further points to make. First, the fact that Jesus is polemical does not give us an excuse to be polemical, and second, we need to think carefully about who the polemic is directed against.

On the first point, it is important to recognise the teaching that Jesus gives about judgement earlier in this Gospel. He says:

"Do not judge, so that you may not be judged. For with the judgement you make you will be judged, and the measure you give will be the measure you get. Why do you see the speck in your neighbour's eye, but do not notice the log in your own eye? Or how can you say to your neighbour, "Let me take the speck out of your eye", while the log is in your own eye? You hypocrite, first take the log out of your own eye, and then you will see clearly to take the speck out of your neighbour's eye (Matthew 7:1-5).

Although the NRSV talks about "neighbours," in the original text Jesus talks about "brothers," or perhaps nowadays we might say "siblings."

Jesus is clear that we are not to judge others, not even those close to us. Sadly, down the years this chapter has been abused to condemn Judaism in general and the Pharisees in particular. This is odd, because the Pharisees were a lay-led purity movement, devoted to hearing what God wanted and putting it into practice in their daily lives. Jesus warns us against judging our fellow siblings in faith, our fellow descendants of Abraham. We ought, rather, to attend to the logs in our own eyes.

And Matthew 23 is actually rather useful in this regard. Bible scholar Donald Hagner is clear that the main contemporary usage of this passage is to critique the Christian church. And if we used in in this way, what challenges might we find?

First, a warning to preachers to only talk about what they actually do, not to create a holier-than-thou image of false piety, but to be appropriately honest and open about the struggles of living a genuine Christian life.

Second, a warning to any in positions of leadership to avoid the seduction of power. I'm very mindful of this and work hard to not inflate my own sense of self-importance. A family who tease me and are at times appropriately robust in stopping me getting full of myself are a great blessing, if a trifle annoying at times.

Third, the risk of setting up of one's own authority as though greater than God's. It's easy for Christians to mock the point about tithing herbs and so become religious hypocrites. As Hilton and Marshall point out, the rabbis worked through lots of nitty-gritty detail in order to anchor the over-arching principles of justice and mercy in the realities of everyday life. Christians might do well to pause and think about where their clothes and food come from, to consider how many people are exploited and abused so we can enjoy cheap clothes, convenient food deliveries and so forth. Paying attention to the impact of our choices is a crucial piece of discipleship.

Fourth, the charge of being whitewashed tombs could all too easily be made against my own denomination, the Anglican church. We may present ourselves as the established Church, headed by the King and so on, but the realities uncovered by the independent inquiry into child sex abuse have made it all too obvious how hypocritical we have been. There is no possibility of pointing fingers at others until we get our own house in order. Religious leaders like to whitewash their sins, but the truth will out.

Fifth, remember, Jesus teaches us that hatred is as bad as murder, so before you feel smug about not murdering prophets, how many godly people have you abused for not sharing your theology? How many people have you condemned for not seeing the world as you do? Judge not, lest you be judged.

And yet, and yet, the Lord is merciful.

Commenting on the final section of the chapter, of the hen who gathers her chicks under her wings, Tom Wright writes: "There have been recorded instances of a mother hen, faced with a fire, collecting her young chickens under her wings to keep them safe. Sometimes she is successful: when the fire has done its worst and died down, you may find a dead hen with live chicks underneath its wings."

Are we not those chicks? God's judgement fell on Jesus on the cross. All those who take shelter under his wings are protected and saved.

Faced with the polemic of this chapter, our response should not be to judge or to imitate, but to listen and to repent. Doubtless more could be said, but for the moment perhaps enough has been.

I'm reminded of the sinner's prayer:

Lord, I see I am more flawed and sinful than I ever dared believe, but that I am even more loved and accepted than I ever dared hope. I turn from my old life of living for myself. I have nothing in my record to merit Your approval, but I now rest in what Jesus did and ask to be accepted into and equipped to live as a member of God's family for his sake. Amen.

Sample sermon on Matthew 27:25

"Why is it that at the very heart of Western culture we're portrayed as the personification of evil?"

That was the reaction of Rabbi Tony Bayfield on listening to Bach's St Matthew Passion at the Royal Festival Hall. It's not that Rabbi Bayfield didn't appreciate the music. Far from it. He says he enjoyed the music, but was devastated, once again, by how Matthew's Gospel portrays "the Jews."

And nowhere has that portrayal been more damaging, more destructive, than in this verse. Doubtless you have heard many sermons on Jesus' trial, listened to, or helped read, the Passion narrative during Holy Week. But have you ever stopped to consider this exchange?

> So when Pilate saw that he could do nothing, but rather that a riot was beginning, he took some water and washed his hands before the crowd, saying, "I am innocent of this man's blood; see to it yourselves." Then the people as a whole answered, "His blood be on us and on our children!" So he released Barabbas for them; and after flogging Jesus, he handed him over to be crucified (Matthew 27:24-26, NRSV).

There are so many fascinating aspects to this text, the history of interpretation has been so destructive, we can only scratch the surface in the next few minutes. I urge you to read more, talk more, pray more about the history of how Christians have abused Jewish people down the centuries. And a lot of it can be traced back to how these verses have been interpreted.

Let's begin with Pilate. He's the highest Roman official in the land, so his is the ultimate authority. You'll recall that earlier in his account, Matthew tells us that Pilate realises Jesus has been handed over because of the jealousy of the Jewish religious authorities, and that Pilate's wife has a dream, which she conveys to her husband, that speaks of Jesus' innocence. Be that as it may, Pilate surely cannot believe what he says here. He is not innocent. Granted, washing your hands is a sign of innocence, attested in Deuteronomy and elsewhere. But Pilate is the one who makes the decision to have Jesus crucified; he bears some of the responsibility, at the very least.

Then let's turn to the crowd, the people as a whole as Matthew describes them. Who are they, and what do they mean when they say, "His blood be on us and on our children!"? First, for who they are. Clearly, they are not all the Jewish people alive at that time, not even all the Jewish people in Jerusalem. Some might have gathered out of curiosity, some out of enmity towards Jesus, who knows. But I expect they made their minds up very quickly. They saw their religious leaders, the people they trusted to show them how to live, the men who explained God's will to them. They saw these people condemn Jesus, accuse him of blasphemy. And they heard nothing from Jesus, no protest, no denial. What would you have thought? Religious authorities whom you trust say this is a bad man, a wicked man, a blasphemer, a danger to you and your children. We want the Romans to do away with him. Would you really have done anything other than agree? There are countless studies that show this is what human beings are like. If a loud, seemingly powerful, vocal minority are confident and clear, if there is no opposition, no dissent, then that is the way things go. Jesus is a blasphemer, he's potential trouble, its best for everyone that he dies. So yes, his blood be on us. God will not mind the death of a blasphemer, the gathered crowd presume.

And what does Matthew mean by those fateful words? What significance does he see in the decision of the crowds? Whether prophecy or recognition after the fact, Matthew sees the destruction of Jerusalem as just punishment on this specific generation. For as you may well remember, the Jewish people rebelled against the might of Rome in 66 CE, a bloody rebellion that culminated in the destruction of Jerusalem, including the temple, in 70 CE. For Matthew and the first generation of Jewish followers of Jesus, this was doubtless divine retribution; just punishment on the people who condemned Jesus to death, on those individuals and their children, no one else, no one more. It was an idea that some rabbis also held, that Jerusalem fell at that time in history because that generation was particularly sinful.

But this is the great sin of the church. We took what is surely a time-limited acceptance of responsibility, and made it universal. When Jewish scholar of the New Testament Amy-Jill Levine was seven, this happened to her:

> A friend on the school bus said to me, "You killed our Lord." "I did not," I responded with some indignation. Deicide would be the sort of thing I would have recalled. "Yes, you did," the girl insisted. "Our priest said so." Apparently, she had been taught that "the Jews" were responsible for the death of Jesus. Since I was the only one she knew, I must be guilty (The Misunderstood Jew, p.2).

Clearly this is nonsense. A seven-year-old American Jewish girl born in the twentieth century, did not kill Jesus. But why was it not clear enough for centuries? Why did the Christian church succumb to racism, to accepting, even encouraging, the pogroms in which countless thousands of innocent Jewish people died?

I think it started with fear, and then migrated into pride, all the time shaped by inhumanity. Matthew and his fellow first-followers of Jesus were probably Jewish, with perhaps some gentiles joining them. They were few in number, faced by overwhelming pressure and odds. They saw nothing wrong in this statement; they may well have theologically agreed with Paul that all people everywhere are culpable for Jesus' death, for all have sinned and fallen short of the glory of God. They probably agreed that socio-politically it was Roman authorities and the Jewish religious elite that manoeuvred things so Jesus died. But they had no power, so they weren't worried about the impact of their words.

But fast forward a few centuries, and the church has power. It is no longer unacceptable to be Christian, indeed it's a route to success. So ambitious people follow Jesus, for mixed motives, like the rest of us. Somewhere in that mix comes condemnation of the Jews. A minority now in comparison to the Christians, an easy target to blame for social ills and what better pretext than to take this bit of Matthew's Gospel. "His blood be upon us," the Jews said, they admit they killed God, so we can, should, kill them.

And centuries of bloody persecution began. Nowadays Western Christians don't kill Jews, don't even blame them for the death of Jesus. But I have heard this idea elsewhere within the Church. And I have seen antisemitism rise in this country and elsewhere. We cannot be complacent, cannot say this is a problem dealt with and it is time to move on.

Christians believe that all are culpable for the death of Jesus in the sense that it was because of human rebellion against God that Jesus emptied himself, taking the form of a slave and becoming obedient unto death. The only singling out we can do within that generality is to admit our own guilt, our own need of salvation. If we are honest, we should, I suggest, admit that if we were in the crowd, we too would have called for Jesus' death and accepted responsibility for his blood being shed. All four Gospels are united in their witness that no one protested at that point, although his mother Mary, disciple John and one or two others were brave enough to witness his death.

When we read this passage, we must admit our guilt, that our sinful selfish, self-interested human nature is the root cause of Jesus' death. And with that admission comes the further recognition of Christian culpability in the death of thousands, maybe even millions, of Jews. It is no easy thing to deal with the failures of the past, but we must try, taking what small steps we can, to build a better world than the one we have inherited.

Lord God, when we think of how Christians have abused your word to justify killing innocent people, we are sorry and ashamed. May your Spirit illuminate our hearts, help us to see where we personally have done wrong in how we have dealt with others. Help us to repent, to change, to build a better world. For your glory and the growth of your kingdom. Amen.

Postscript

This book has explored the attitudes towards Jewish people that are found within Matthew's Gospel. The focus has been on the so-called "blood cry" of 27:25, which has been used throughout history as the foundation upon which to build the charge of deicide against the Jewish people. It is the contention of this book that this is a false foundation. Matthew's Gospel does not condemn Jewish people in general, nor does it single them out as culpable for deicide.

Chapter one provided an overview and orientation within relevant academic debates concerning Matthew's Gospel. Chapter two explored what Matthew means by Jesus being the "fulfilment" of the Jewish law. This introduced the central interpretative challenge for Christians; how can we say God is doing a new work in and through Jesus without condemning, appropriating or replacing what he has done and continues to do in and through Jewish people? Chapter three discussed the nature and function of polemic within ancient texts. It was noted that recognising certain passages in Matthew are polemical constitutes a necessary, but insufficient, explanation. It was also argued that the polemic should be read as indicating opponents existed, but the detail should not necessarily be understood as an objective, accurate portrayal of them. We must recognise the damaging impact of polemic and develop appropriate interpretations in response.

Chapter four discussed Matthew 23 and chapter five a single verse, 27:25. These two chapters explored how best to limit the scope of the polemic, arguing that internal focus is the best interpretative strategy. That is to say, the critique of the Pharisees in Matthew 23 can be redirected as a critique of the Christian church, focusing specifically on one's own context and actions. Likewise, the acceptance of responsibility for the death of Jesus is a personal one. The Christian believes that I am the one for whom Jesus died, and so I am the one who accepts culpability for his blood. It is not my place to judge or condemn others for the choices that they make.

Chapter six discussed blood libels, arguing that the plausibility of the charge of ritual murder is founded upon a mistaken belief that "the Jews killed Jesus." Christians must recognise this sorry history and learn from it, as it continues to spread to this day. Chapter seven proposed ways for Christians to preach and teach with Jewish people in mind. Chapter eight put those suggestions into practice through four sample sermons.

The central question this book asks is, who is responsible for the death of Jesus? In the preface I argued that Matthew's Gospel teaches us that Jesus takes responsibility for his own death, setting his face towards Jerusalem, and accepting what happened there because he believed that in doing so, healing and hope might enter the world. For Christians, who believes that Jesus died for them, it is also important to own personal responsibility for Jesus' death. We believe that Jesus, through his death, dealt with all our shame and shortcomings. One of the great failures of Christians down the centuries has been to inaccurately hold all Jewish people for all time culpable for Jesus' death. Of this, and much else, we have cause to repent, to turn away from. I hope this book can play its own small part in encouraging Christians to preach and teach the Christian Gospel in such a way that it is heard as bringing good news. And whether it is accepted or rejected, to love those they encounter as they love themselves.

References

Archbishops' Council. 2019. *God's Unfailing Word: Theological and Practical Perspectives on Christian-Jewish Relations.* London: Church House Publishing.

Bauckham, Richard. 2017. *Jesus and the Eyewitnesses: The Gospels as Eyewitness Testimony.* Second Edition. Grand Rapids: Eerdmans.

Bayfield, Tony (Ed.). 2017. *Deep Calls to Deep: Transforming Conversations between Jews and Christians.* London: SCM Press.

Beaton, Richard. 2002. *Isaiah's Christ in Matthew's Gospel.* Society for New Testament Studies Monograph Series 123. Cambridge: Cambridge University Press.

Berenson, Edward. 2019. *The Accusation: Blood Libel in an American Town.* New York: W W Norton.

Borowsky, Irvin J. 1996. "Foreword: The Language of Religion" in Kee, Howard Clark and Irvin J. Borowsky (Eds). *Removing Anti-Judaism from the Pulpit.* New York: Continuum, pp.7-10.

Boyarin, D. 2004. *Borderlines: The Partition of Judaeo-Christianity.* Philadelphia: University of Pennsylvania Press.

Callaway, Mary C. 1993. "A Hammer That Breaks Rocks in Pieces: Prophetic Critique in the Hebrew Bible" in Evans, Craig A. and Donald A. Hagner (Eds). *Anti-Semitism and Early Christianity: Issues of Polemic and Faith.* Minneapolis: Augsburg Fortress Press, pp.21-38.

Carter, Warren. 2007. "Matthews' Gospel: An Anti-Imperial/Imperial Reading" *Currents in Theology and Mission* 34:6.

CCJ. 2020. *Listening and Learning: Dialogue between Christians and Jews on issues relating to Israel-Palestine.* London: Council of Christians and Jews. Available from https://ccj.org.uk/resources/israel-palestine-dialogue.

Chazan, Robert. 2016. *From Anti-Judaism to Anti-Semitism: Ancient and Medieval Christian Constructions of Jewish History.* Cambridge: Cambridge University Press.

Chilton, Bruce and Jacob Neusner. 1995. *Judaism in the New Testament: Practices and Beliefs.* London: Routledge.

Colson, F. H. 1971. *The Embassy to Gaius*. Cambridge: Harvard University Press.

Crossley James G. 2020. "Matthew and the Torah: Jesus as Legal Interpreter" in Runesson, Anders and Daniel M. Gurtner (Eds). *Matthew within Judaism: Israel and the Nations in the First Gospel*. Atlanta: SBL Press, pp.29-52.

Daly, Robert J. 1996. "Removing Anti-Judaism from the Pulpit: Four Approaches" in Kee, Howard Clark and Irvin J. Borowsky (Eds). *Removing Anti-Judaism from the Pulpit*. New York: Continuum, pp.50-59.

Dunn, J. D. G. 2003. *Jesus Remembered: Christianity in the Making Volume 1*. Grand Rapids: Eerdmans.

Dunn, J. D. G. 2006. *The Partings of the Ways: Between Christianity and Judaism and their Significance for the Character of Christianity*. Second Edition. London: SCM Press.

Florence, Ronald 2004. *Blood Libel: The Damascus Affair of 1840*. Wisconsin: University of Wisconsin Press.

France, R. T. 1989. *Matthew: Evangelist and Teacher*. Carlisle: Paternoster.

France, R. T. 2007. *The Gospel of Matthew: New International Commentary on the New Testament*. Grand Rapids: Eerdmans.

Fredriksen, Paula. 2002. "The Birth of Christianity and the Origins of Christian Anti-Judaism" in Fredrikesen, Paula and Adele Reinhartz (Eds). *Jesus, Judaism and Christian anti-Judaism*. Louisville: Westminster John Knox, pp.8-30.

Gale, Aaron M. 2005. *Redefining Ancient Borders: The Jewish Scribal Framework of Matthew's Gospel*. London: T & T Clark.

Gale, Aaron M. 2017. *The Gospel According to Matthew* in Levine, Amy-Jill and Marc Zvi Brettler (Eds). *The Jewish Annotated New Testament*. Second Edition. Oxford: Oxford University Press, pp.9-66.

Gerdmar, A. 2009. *Roots of Theological Anti-Semitism*. Leiden: Brill.

Goldsmith, Martin. 2001. *Matthew and Mission: The Gospel Through Jewish Eyes*. Carlisle: Paternoster.

Grunwald-Spier, Agnes. 2016. *Who Betrayed the Jews? The Realities of Nazi persecution in the Holocaust*. Cheltenham: The History Press.

Hagner, Donald. 1993. *Matthew 1 – 13 Word Biblical Commentary*. Dallas: Word Books.

Hagner, Donald. 1995. *Matthew 14 – 28 Word Biblical Commentary*. Dallas: Word Books.

Harrington, Daniel J. 2007. "Problems and Opportunities in Matthew's Gospel." *Currents in Theology and Mission* 34 (6) 417-23.

Heil, John Paul. 1991. *The Death and Resurrection of Jesus: A Narrative-Critical Reading of Matthew 26-28*. Minneapolis: Fortress Press.

Hilton, Michael and Gordian Marshall. 1988. *The Gospels and Rabbinic Judaism: A Study Guide*. London: SCM Press.

Holmgren, Frederick C. "Preaching the Gospel without Anti-Judaism" in Kee, Howard Clark and Irvin J. Borowsky (Eds). *Removing Anti-Judaism from the Pulpit*. New York: Continuum, pp.67-74.

Isaac, E. 1983. "1 (Ethiopic Apocalypse of) Enoch" in James H Charlesworth (Ed). *The Old Testament Pseudepigrapha Volume 1*. New York: Anchor Bible, pp.5-89.

Johnson, Luke T. 1989. "The New Testament's Anti-Jewish slander and the conventions of Ancient Polemic." *Journal of Biblical Literature*. 108 (3) 419-441.

Kampen, John. 2019. *Matthew within Sectarian Judaism*. New Haven: Yale University Press.

Kampen, John. 2020. "The Problem of Christian Anti-Semitism and a Sectarian Reading of the Gospel of Matthew: The Trial of Jesus" in Runesson, Anders and Daniel M. Gurtner (Eds). *Matthew within Judaism: Israel and the Nations in the First Gospel*. Atlanta: SBL Press, pp.371-97.

Kee, Howard Clark 1983. "Testaments of the Twelve Patriarchs" in James H Charlesworth (Ed). *The Old Testament Pseudepigrapha Volume 1*. New York: Anchor Bible, pp.775-828.

Kee, Howard Clark and Irvin J. Borowsky (Eds). 1996. *Removing Anti-Judaism from the Pulpit*. New York: Continuum.

Keener, Craig. 1999. *A Commentary on the Gospel of Matthew*. Grand Rapids: Eerdmans.

Klijn, A F J. 1983. "2 (Syriac Apocalypse of) Baruch" in James H Charlesworth (Ed). *The Old Testament Pseudepigrapha Volume 1* New York: Anchor Bible, pp.615-52.

Konradt, Matthias. 2020. "The Role of the Crowds in the Gospel of Matthew" in Runesson, Anders and Daniel M. Gurtner (Eds). *Matthew within Judaism: Israel and the Nations in the First Gospel*. Atlanta: SBL Press, pp.213-31.

Le Donne, Anthony and Larry Behrendt. 2017. *Sacred Dissonance: The Blessing of Difference in Jewish-Christian Dialogue*. Peabody: Hendrickson Publishers.

Levin, Edmund. 2014. *A Child of Christian Blood: Murder and Conspiracy in Tsarist Russia: The Beilis Blood Libel*. New York: Schocken Books.

Levine, Amy-Jill. 1988. *The Social and Ethical Dimensions of Matthean Salvation History: "Go nowhere among the Gentiles…" (Matt 10:5b). Studies in the Bible and Early Christianity 14*. Lewiston, NY: Edwin Mellen Press.

Levine, Amy-Jill. 2002. "Matthew, Mark, and Luke: Good News or Bad? in Fredrikesen, Paula and Adele Reinhartz (Eds). *Jesus, Judaism and Christian anti-Judaism*. Louisville: Westminster John Knox, pp.77-98.

Levine, Amy-Jill. 2006. *The Misunderstood Jew: The Church and the Scandal of the Jewish Jesus*. New York: HarperOne.

Levine, Amy-Jill. 2021. "Preaching and Teaching the Pharisees" in Sievers, Joseph and Amy-Jill Levine (Eds). *The Pharisees*. Grand Rapids: Eerdmans, pp.403-27.

Levine, Amy-Jill. 2022. "Supersessionism: Admit and Address Rather than Debate or Deny" *Insights and Issues in the ongoing Jewish-Christian Dialogue*. International Council of Christians and Jews 2022. Available at https://www.jcrelations.net/article/supersessionism-admit-and-address-rather-than-debate-or-deny.html

Levine, Amy-Jill and Marc Zvi Brettler. 2020. *The Bible with and without Jesus: How Jews and Christians Read the Same Stories Differently*. New York: Harper One.

Lipton, Sara. 2014. *Dark Mirror: The Medieval Origins of Anti-Jewish Iconography*. New York: Metropolitan Books.

Malamud, Bernard. 1966. *The Fixer*. London: Penguin Books.

Martínez, Florentino García and Eibert J C Tigchelaar. 1997. *The Dead Sea Scrolls Study Edition Volume 1 (1Q1-4Q273)*. Leiden: Brill.

Marty, Martin E. 1996. "Removing Anti-Judaism from the Christian Pulpit" in Kee, Howard Clark and Irvin J. Borowsky (Eds). *Removing Anti-Judaism from the Pulpit*. New York: Continuum, pp.15-28.

Mayfield, Tyler D. 2020. *Unto Us a Son is Born: Isaiah, Advent, and Our Jewish Neighbors*. Grand Rapids: Eerdmans.

Mayfield, Tyler D. 2022. *Father Abraham's Many Children: The Bible in a World of Religious Difference*. Grand Rapids: Eerdmans.

Metzger, B. M. 1983. "The Fourth Book of Ezra" in James H Charlesworth (Ed). *The Old Testament Pseudepigrapha Volume 1*. New York: Anchor Bible, pp.517-59.

Morrison, Craig E. 2021. "Interpreting the Name 'Pharisee'" in Sievers, Joseph and Amy-Jill Levine (Eds). *The Pharisees*. Grand Rapids: Eerdmans, pp.3-19.

Neusner, Jacob. 1984. *Judaism in the beginning of Christianity*. London: SPCK.

Nolland, John. 2005. *The Gospel of Matthew: A Commentary on the Greek Text. The New International Greek Testament Commentary*. Grand Rapids: Eerdmans.

Overman, J. Andrew. 1990. *Matthew's Gospel and Formative Judaism: The Social World of the Matthean Community*. Minneapolis: Fortress Press.

Overman, J. Andrew. 1996. *Church and Community in Crisis: The Gospel According to Matthew*. Valley Forge: Trinity Press International.

Quarles, Charles L. 2021. "The Oath Formulas of Matthew 23:16-22 as Evidence for a Pre-70 Date of Composition for Matthew's Gospel." *Tyndale Bulletin* 72:1-24.

Rose, E M. 2015. *The Murder of William of Norwich: The Origins of the Blood Libel in Medieval Europe*. Oxford: Oxford University Press.

Rittner, Carol, Stephen D. Smith and Irena Steinfeldt (Eds). 2000. *The Holocaust and the Christian World*. London: Kuperard.

Rubin, Miri. 2014. *The Life and Passion of William of Norwich by Thomas of Monmouth*. London: Penguin.

Ruether, Rosemary. 1997. *Faith and Fratricide: The Theological Roots of Anti-Semitism* Eugene: Wipf and Stock.

Runesson, Anders and Daniel M. Gurtner (Eds). 2020. *Matthew within Judaism: Israel and the Nations in the First Gospel*. Atlanta: SBL Press.

Ryan, Jordan. 2020. "The Sermon on the Mount as Synagogue Teaching" in Runesson, Anders and Daniel M. Gurtner (Eds). *Matthew within Judaism: Israel and the Nations in the First Gospel*. Atlanta: SBL Press, pp.53-73.

Saldarini, Anthony J. 1994. *Matthew's Christian-Jewish Community*. Chicago: University of Chicago Press.

Sawyer, John F A. 1996. *The Fifth Gospel: Isaiah in the History of Christianity*. Cambridge: Cambridge University Press.

Schiffman, Lawrene H. 2017. "Pharisees" in Levine, Amy-Jill and Marc Zvi Brettler (Eds). *The Jewish Annotated New Testament*. Second Edition. Oxford: Oxford University Press, pp.619-22.

Schwartz, Daniel R. 2017. "Jewish Movements of the New Testament Period," in Levine, Amy-Jill and Marc Zvi Brettler (Eds). *The Jewish Annotated New Testament*. Second Edition. Oxford: Oxford University Press, pp.614-19.

Sider-Hamilton, Catherine. 2008. "'His Blood be upon Us' Innocent Blood and the Death of Jesus in Matthew." *Catholic Biblical Quarterly* 70: 82-100.

Stemberger, Günter. 2000. "The Formation of Rabbinic Judaism, 70-640 CE" in Neusner, Jacob and Alan J. Avery-Peck (Eds). *The Blackwell Companion to Judaism*. Oxford: Blackwell, pp.78-92.

Stemberger, Günter. 2021. "The Pharisees and the Rabbis" in Sievers, Joseph and Amy-Jill Levine (Eds). *The Pharisees*. Grand Rapids: Eerdmans, pp.240-54.

Teter, Magda. 2020. *Blood Libel: On the Trail of an Antisemitic Myth*. Cambridge: Harvard University Press.

Thackeray, H. St J. 1926. *Josephus' Life*. Cambridge: Harvard University Press.

Wilken, Robert. 1983. *John Chrysostom and the Jews: Rhetoric and Reality in the late Fourth Century*. Eugene: Wipf and Stock.

Williamson, Clark M. and Ronald J. Allen. 1996. "Interpreting Difficult Texts" in Kee, Howard Clark and Irvin J. Borowsky (Eds). *Removing Anti-Judaism from the Pulpit*. New York: Continuum, pp.36-42.

Wilson, Tom. 2019. *Hospitality, Service, Proclamation: Interfaith Engagement as Christian Discipleship*. London: SCM Press.

Wilson, Tom. 2020. *Jesus and the Ioudaioi: Reading John's Gospel with Jewish People in Mind*. Newcastle-upon-Tyne: Cambridge Scholars Publishing.

Wright, N. T. 1993. *The New Testament and the People of God*. London: SPCK.

Wright, N. T. 1997. *Jesus and the Victory of God*. London: SPCK.

Wright, N. T. 2002a. *Matthew for Everyone*. Part 1. Chapters 1-15. London: SPCK.

Wright, N. T. 2002b. *Matthew for Everyone*. Part 2. Chapters 16-28. London: SPCK.

Wright, N. T. 2003. *The Resurrection of the Son of God*. London: SPCK.

Wright, N. T. 2013a. *Paul and the Faithfulness of God. Parts I and II.* London: SPCK.

Wright, N. T. 2013b. *Paul and the Faithfulness of God. Parts III and IV.* London: SPCK.

Wright, R B. 1985. "Psalms of Solomon" in James H Charlesworth (Ed). *The Old Testament Pseudepigrapha Volume 2.* New York: Anchor Bible, pp.639-70.

Yarbro-Collins, Adela. 2021. "Polemic against the Pharisees in Matthew 23" in Sievers, Joseph and Amy-Jill Levine (Eds). *The Pharisees.* Grand Rapids: Eerdmans, pp.148-69.

Lightning Source UK Ltd.
Milton Keynes UK
UKHW031955241022
411033UK00002B/35

9 781804 410745